21X 10/07 ✓10/07
29X 4/13 ✓ 5/13

D0689197

Sister Surfer

OCT 1 1 2005

Sister Surfer

A Woman's Guide to Surfing with Bliss and Courage

by Kia Afcari and Mary Osborne

The Lyons Press
Guilford, Connecticut
An imprint of The Globe Pequot Press

Note: Before you begin any exercise program, it is strongly recommended that you consult your physician. Execute proper form during all exercises and stretches. If you experience dizziness, pain, or discomfort, stop immediately and consult with your physician.

To buy books in quantity for corporate use or incentives, call **(800) 962–0973, ext. 4551,** or e-mail **premiums@GlobePequot.com.**

Copyright © 2005 by Kia Arcari and Mary Osborne

Illustration credits: Erik Tieze: 19, 25, 39, 40, 41, 79, 80; Pepin Press, Agile Rabbit Editions (used throughout): vi, xiii, 1, 4; Photos.com (used throughout): v. Photo credits: Kia Afcari: 5, 13 (bottom), 16, 32, 122, 124, 125, 127-132, 134-136, 138, 139, 149 (Janine headshot), 163; Brand X Pictures: viii-ix, 27, 51, 58-59, 92-93, 147, 155; EyeWire: 114; Elizabeth Pepin: 3, 15, 31(top), 35, 47, 56, 61, 62, 68-70, 72, 76, 78, 81, 83, 89, 90, 95, 97, 98-102, 104, 106-108, 110-113, 116, 143, 144, 148 (Kia headshot), 156, 159, 164; Photos.com: xi, xiii, 6, 36, 46, 57, 167; PhotoDisc: xiv, 2, 9, 30, 43, 115, 163; David Pu'u: xviii-xix, 10-11, 28-29, 44-45, 66-67, 75, 120-121, 137, 140-141, 148 (Mary headshot); Chris Sanders: 149 (Bev headshot); David Silva: 149 (Elizabeth headshot); Annie Tritt: xii, 8, 13(top), 27, 42, 82, 149 (Liane headshot); Steve Wilkings: v.

ALL RIGHTS RESERVED. No part of this book may be reproduced or transmitted in any form by any means, electronic or mechanical, including photocopying and recording, or by any information storage and retrieval system, except as may be expressly permitted in writing from the publisher. Requests for permission should be addressed to The Lyons Press, Attn: Rights and Permissions Department, P.O. Box 480, Guilford, CT 06437.

The Lyons Press is an imprint of The Globe Pequot Press

10 9 8 7 6 5 4 3 2 1

Printed in the United States of America

Designed by LeAnna Weller Smith

Library of Congress Cataloging-in-Publication Data
Afcari, Kia.
    Sister surfer : a woman's guide to surfing with bliss and courage / by Kia Afcari and Mary Osborne.
      p. cm.
  Includes bibliographical references and index.
    ISBN 1-59228-721-2 (trade paper : alk. paper)
      1. Surfing for women. 2. Women surfers. I. Osborne, Mary. II. Title.
GV839.7.W65A43 2005
797.3'2'082--dc22
                                    2005003122

Dedication

If you surf on the north shore of Oahu, you can feel the Queen of Makaha. Her essence is physically present among the warmth of earth tones and in the hiss of waves. Her ashes were spread there by hundreds of well-wishers who, after fifteen years of watching her battle breast cancer, paddled out into the surf to bid her farewell. Conch shells were blown, poi was made, and people washed their tears into the sea that so loved Rell.

People who don't even know Rell have been changed by her. Her Hawaiian name, K'apio Lokea Ula, means *the heart of the sea*. Which is exactly what she was. She was our heart to the ocean, oxidizing our blood by bringing us aloha, circulating the life force that moved so many. Rell helped every little *keiki* within miles to reclaim the ocean as their playground. Her mere existence inspired women, worldwide.

Today we spread this book into the seas in the spirit of Rell, a message in a bottle for women.

Mahalo, **Auntie Rell.**

table of contents

Acknowledgments

FROM MARY OSBORNE . . .

Special thanks to everyone who helped make this book happen:

- My mother and father, for creating me and guiding me through my crazy lifestyle.
- My three brothers, Sean, Ryan, and David, for influencing me in every way possible and pushing me to higher limits while out in the water. I would never have picked up a surfboard if it weren't for you three.
- David Pu'u, for working with me from day one, teaching me so much about the surf industry, and creating such breathtaking photographs.
- To all my surf sponsors, for believing in me and allowing me to follow my dreams and goals.
- To the crew at Creative Artists Agency, thank you for helping me in every way possible.
- To all the strong and powerful women who dedicated their time to this book. You are all such influential human beings and amazing role models.
- Deidre Knight and Ann Treistman—you both made this become a reality.
- Kia Afcari—this book wouldn't have been created without you. Thank you for asking me to be a part of it!

FROM KIA AFCARI . . .

I'd like to acknowledge all the wonderful women who made this project possible:

- Mary Osborne, whose openness and positive energy brings her abundance.
- Yasmeen Mussard-Afcari, my daughter, for your encouragement and wonderful spirit.
- Elizabeth Pepin—your gorgeous photographs and hard work made this book possible.
- Annie Tritt, for your wonderful portraits and photojournalism.
- Bev Sanders—your wonderful Las Olas stories brought me to tears.
- Liane Louie, for your incredible story, your insights on psychology, and your unfailing encouragement.
- Janine Daley, for sharing your vast knowledge about fitness.
- Isabelle Mussard, for getting me here.
- Moji Afcari, a sister, a surfer, and one of the most loving people I know.
- Sima Afcari, for always having big dreams for me.
- Tanya Cruz Teller, for being so Tanya.
- Cheryl Larsen, for your inspiring story, deep courage, and excitement about the book.
- Maura Wolf and www.mindwing.org, for your deep insight and fabulous coaching.
- Renée Swindle, a wonderful writer, for your sharp and mindful editing.

- Leslie Kirk Campbell and www.ripefruitwriting. com, for the writing faith.
- Natalie Goldberg, for your phenomenal book, *Writing Down the Bones.*
- Charlotte LaGarde, for the inspiration of your stunning movie, *Heart of the Sea.*
- Nani Naish, for your fabulous stories and aloha.
- Zeuf, for living a life that moves us and sharing that life so freely.
- Mary Bagalso, a wonderful person and an epic surfer.
- Tais Kintgen and Susana Souza Franca, "*Muitos obrigadós para todos!*"
- Lauri Black, for inspiring us with that belly.
- Izzy Tihanyi, for your openness and belief in abundance.
- Deidre Knight of the Knight Agency, for your unbridled enthusiasm and dedication to this project.
- Ann Treistman, for your editing prowess and for helping us make this real.

I'd also like to thank the men who assisted in this project: my father, Mohamed Afcari, a seaman who always shared his love for the ocean; Ameer Mussard-Afcari, a very cool little boy; Moses Yao, for the wonderful mandalas; Andy Sundblad and www.screenres.net, for the wonderful web design; David Pu'u, for your gorgeous photos; Chris Sanders, for all the help with the Las Olas archives.

And to all the people of Itacaré, Bahia, Brazil, who showed me paradise.

Introduction

A SURFER'S LIFE

I was raised with my three older brothers on the beautiful beach of Solimar in Ventura, California. Being the only girl, my mother dreamed of having a daughter who was a perfect ballerina. I was enrolled in ballet and jazz classes and was even a cheerleader in high school. With my father's influence, I was involved in sports like volleyball and basketball. I tried every kind of dance class and played every sport known to mankind, but I knew something was missing.

We lived near the beach, and my brothers and I played constantly in the water and on the sand. I watched them surf every day while I made sandcastles on the shoreline. I eventually discovered the body board, which enabled me to go into the water and learn about riding the waves on my belly. Body boarding was fun—but I still wanted to go surfing with my brothers and their friends and be like them. At the age of fifteen, I picked up my first surfboard. My older brother David paddled with me to the outside lineup and helped me paddle into my first wave. I remember catching the wave and riding it into shore, my brother surfing right next to me. I was thrilled—and from that day forward, I knew surfing was going to be a big part of my life.

I saved up $180 from babysitting to buy my first surfboard from a local surf shop. I bought a seven-foot, fun-shaped board, and I rode until I could not ride it anymore. My goal was to be better than all the boys I grew up with. I wanted to prove that girls could be just as good as the boys. Surfing eventually took over my extracurricular activities at school, and I no longer wanted to play team sports. I wanted to become a professional surfer.

At the age of sixteen, I started working in a surf shop where I was lucky enough to meet surfboard shaper and surf photographer David Pu'u. I saw an ad in *Surfer* magazine, calling for surf shots of female surfers. David and I worked together to create beautiful images that were eventually sent out to several surf magazines. I remember seeing my first photo in *Longboard* magazine. I was shocked with excitement and wanted another one. I began to promote myself by attending trade shows, contacting companies, and competing in surf contests up and down the coast. My name eventually began to grow, and magazines started writing articles about me.

I just kept on surfing. The only change was people started recognizing me. The best compliments I get today are from children and their parents, telling me I am a good role model. I never really looked at surfing like that. It was just something I did for fun. But now that so many young girls surf, I'm honored to be a positive role model for them.

After earning my associate's degree, I went back to earn a bachelor's degree. I barely made it through one whole semester. I was so frustrated with everything in my life. I was trying to juggle ten things at once: I needed to get rid of something before my plate overflowed. I decided to drop out of school and, coincidentally, the day I left I received a phone call informing me I was selected to participate in the MTV reality show, *Surf Girls*. I wasn't sure what I was getting myself into. But at this point in my life, it sounded amazing.

Filming the reality show was an interesting time in my life. I packed my bags for two and a half months, said good-bye to my family, and left not knowing what I was about to encounter. Up until then, I had only dreamed about surfing all over the world. To film the show, I traveled with fourteen women and about forty crew members to Australia, Samoa, Tahiti, Hawaii, and Costa Rica to surf exotic beaches. I felt so lucky to be picked as a participant from thousands of girls. I met fantastic people from all over the world, surfed every

day at new surf spots, and stayed in luxurious hotels that I probably will never stay in again.

I will never forget this time in my life. So many funny, strange, and exciting things were happening to me. One day I would be in a four-star hotel in New York attending a red carpet event; the next day I would be camping on a friend's couch. There was never a dull moment. It was all one big learning experience—and I thanked God every day for giving me the opportunity to grow and fulfill my dreams. I figured I would try to ride the "reality TV wave" as long as possible.

It's not always easy to make it financially as a surfer. Luckily, I have great sponsors who pay me. A surfer can have several endorsements, as long as they're not conflicting products: clothing, shoes, watches, energy drinks, surfboards, etc. Amateurs only get paid if a photo runs in a magazine with visibility of the product or the company's logo; this is called *photo incentive*. When you turn professional, the arrangement changes and the company pays you a yearly salary. Sometimes you have good months and sometimes you have bad months—just like any other job. When I am home for long periods of time, I try to work side jobs to make extra money: work as a nanny, in a restaurant, in an office. You name it, I'll do it. I have to pay the bills.

Unfortunately, it's harder to make it as a woman in the surfing business. Many women surfers make far less money than the men do; it's rare for a top woman surfer to earn the same money as a top male surfer. With the increasing growth and massive population of women in surfing, I would like to say this will change. But only time will tell.

In terms of health and fitness, I am not a big fan of the gym. I don't like being indoors for long periods of time, but I recently started a new core training program geared for surfers and I love it. My main concern is to maintain a healthy lifestyle by eating well and staying active. I believe the best training for surfing is surfing. You use completely different muscles than in any other sport. And surfing is wonderful for your mind, body, and soul.

It has taken a lot of time, practice, and commitment, but I have finally accomplished many of the goals I set for myself. I think my wave of success has not yet ended because I don't ever want it to stop. I'm constantly working to keep my career moving and to keep myself busy. I have worked on music videos, television, modeling jobs, and magazines.

I am finally living the dream I created the day I caught my first wave—and that dream now goes far beyond what I ever imagined. My whole life revolves around surfing. I still get as excited as a kid in a candy store when I catch a first-class ride all the way to shore. It's the best feeling in the world. My memories of the greatest days in my life all revolve around the beach and the ocean. I feel so fortunate to be a surfer, and I hope that one day I can share this lifestyle with my children.

I wanted to write this book with Kia to share the surfing lifestyle. Surfing has given me a sense of security, ambition, motivation, and thrill. It is so easy to learn to surf and to fall in love with the sport. Surfing was once a male-dominated sport, but that has slowly changed. Women from all over the world are now surfing and loving it. This book will inspire, teach, and help other women overcome any fears related to surfing. I hope it brings you happiness in your everyday life—and I hope you experience the same feelings I did when I rode my first wave, and every wave since.

Mary Osborne   Ventura, California

Sister Surfer

CHAPTER 1

AN INVITATION

WHY SHOULD A WOMAN SURF?

Why should a woman surf? Why should a woman do anything? The word *should* has been a dangerous one in the history of women. There have been a billion of them, piled like Irish boulders on women's shoulders: a dress-nice should, a look-pretty should, a lose-weight should. These are the same shoulds that have kept women "in their place." Let's forget the shoulds.

you are doing the impossible you are standing on moving water

Why would a woman surf? Why would a woman eat Belgian chocolate? Make love? Stay in bed all morning long? Because it's incredibly delicious, that's why.

Imagine the feeling of water on your skin . . . being close enough to feel the energy of a wave. You paddle forward, muscles straining, as the wave slowly tries to pull you backward.

You feel the wave slowly lifting you, like a gentle King Kong—the steepness increasing, the hesitation palpable. Spray and wind kiss your face and you feel yourself sliding down the glassy wave. You push up and slide your feet under your body as you stand and drop downward, into the wave. Organs are falling and a feeling of glee penetrates your body, like the time you rode your bike down that big hill, your pigtails flying. You are standing, instinctually turning, as whitewater chases you. You stroke the line of the wave with your hand and tuck down for balance. You carve a graceful line across the wave—leaning, shifting your weight, leaning again. When the energy has passed you lead your board up and over the top of the wave and finish with arms raised, Mary Lou Retton style.

Your smile begins to grow as you realize that at this moment, there is nothing else in the world. You are doing the impossible. You are standing on moving water.

A woman would surf if she had a quiet yearning to be close to the sea.

A woman would surf if she saw her friend's face as she emerged from the water on a cold

Surfing sure is fun. Mary Bagalso
and Summer Romero yukking it up.

September day. Her neurons blasting, blood vessels booming, screaming their aliveness into the ether. Her eyes, marinated in brine, shining in blue-green. Her hair dripping salt water. Her body shivering and teeth chattering. If you saw that look on her face when she stood up on her board, that expression of victory, of defying the huge bay of "I can't," then your eyes would widen and you'd say, "I want that!"

A woman would surf if she needed practice in conquering, in vanquishing fear demons, I-can't demons, limitation demons. A woman might surf if she wanted a no-fail daily meditation practice, minus the boredom. She might surf because she wants to feel as strong as the sea or as calm as the breeze. She might surf if she wants a doorway to possibility. Opening this door, she fulfills one desire—creating evidence that other things are possible.

A woman might surf if, in a moment of despair, she realizes her life is a dreadful bore and she needs to pursue pleasure.

Surfing is not for everyone, but it might be for you. In fact, it might be the one thing that brings you to the life you've always wanted.

HOW TO USE THIS BOOK

This book is designed to remove every barrier, whether psychological or practical, to get you out there surfing. Just like a surf lesson, it starts gently and moves slowly to more specific instruction.

By tackling both the psychological and practical barriers to surfing, *Sister Surfer* covers every-thing—from how to conquer your fear to how to wax your surfboard.

It begins with an invitation to the ocean. In the pages that follow, you'll get inspiration and advice from interviews with a diverse group of surfers, ranging from eight to forty-two years in age. We'll discuss everything from fear to basic topics like how to choose a surf school, how to put on a wetsuit, and what to do when you get to the beach. *Sister Surfer* then covers, in detail, the how-to of surfing: from how to bail without getting hurt to how to look fabulous on a wave. The book ends with a discussion on surfing and liberation and a list of resources for women surfers.

This book will help you get into the ocean and get on a surfboard. Take it to the beach with you and dip a toe in. Contact one of the surf schools listed in the back. Ask a girlfriend or a book club to read this book with you. Whatever helps you open up to the possibility of becoming a surfer is a good thing.

Surfing has huge potential to change your life: the transformational power of the sport is limitless. This book is your first step. It is an invitation to do something absolutely wonderful for yourself. After all, don't you deserve that?

BUILDING A RELATION-SHIP WITH SURFING

Before we get into the nuts and bolts—how to put your surf leash on, how to paddle into a wave—think about why you've chosen to learn how to surf. You know how some of the most challenging

A quiet moment with Yasmeen Mussard-Afcari and her surfboard.

"The sea, the sea, the shining sea . . .
the clean, the fresh, the every free . . ."—Anonymous

relationships teach you about yourself? Your relationship with surfing can be like that. It is a challenging sport that holds many opportunities for growth and self-reflection.

For some of us, becoming a surfer is a natural progression of how we see ourselves. For others, trying something so different is a major step. Understanding why you've chosen to surf will help

you build a cherished relationship with the sport that could last a lifetime.

What is surfing? Is it a joyous, carefree sport for bubbly girls or a serious, extreme sport for the hard-core woman in all of us? The answer is, it's both. Surfing touches each of us in a different way.

Surfing provides us with an opportunity to explore our carefree selves and our courageous

selves. Speaking with dozens of women who are drawn to surfing, we came to understand that these women chose surfing as a way to address something in their lives that needed attention. They chose surfing, whether consciously or subconsciously, as a training ground for self-improvement.

For example, in the interview with forty-two-year-old Cheryl Larsen (see page 42), you'll learn how this woman's simultaneous deep fear and deep desire for the ocean became a metaphor for her life. She knew that if she could conquer her fear of the ocean, she could also conquer the fear of changing careers in mid-life, or the fear of living the life she's always wanted. "Just speaking about the waves would bring up great anxiety for me. . . . But at some point I began to realize that I had to go to the core of my fear. Tackling this core allowed me to open up in ways I never thought possible," she says.

For Dr. Liane Louie (turn to page 8 for our interview with her), a small fear and a desire to reconnect with her Hawaiian roots became the driving force that brought her to surfing. Surfing allowed her to reconstruct a new image of who she was—or who she could be. At times in our lives, we feel stuck in our own molds. But in reality, the choices we have about how to live our lives are limitless. Liane learned that after she tried surfing. "I'm going to hike Half Dome . . . ," she said. "I even went fly-fishing! I've never done stuff like that!"

The idea here is to find out how to make the canvas of our lives continuously empty—to learn how to approach each day as a blank slate, open to any possibility. How do we lose the cornrows of the past, the deep tracks we've dug on a day-to-day basis that keep us bound to the conventions of who we have been and who we are *supposed* to be? For example, if you see yourself as a timid person, that's a message you've heard or a mold you've built for yourself. The reality is, if you lost your fear—whether you're six or sixty—you could develop the skills or attributes needed for any endeavor.

For some of the women profiled in this book, tragedy or a deep struggle was the wake-up call that got them out there on those cold mornings to go surfing. For Liane, her wake-up call was her boyfriend's bout with cancer.

For others, surfing was simply the manifestation of a deep desire to live a different lifestyle—a lifestyle where fun and communion with nature are a priority.

Why have you chosen surfing? Is it because you've forgotten how to have fun? Is it because—whether you're a daughter, mother, girlfriend, or wife—it's been too long since you did something that was all about you? It could take years of wipeouts to be any good at surfing—and maybe you need practice in sticking with something when the going gets tough. Maybe you'd like to conquer some fear in your life. Or maybe you've realized that most of your days are dominated by freeways, cubicles, and fluorescent lights, and you want the free-flowing feeling of water on your skin.

Whatever your reasons, allow yourself the possibility of living each day as a blank canvas. Allow yourself to smash every mold you or others have made for you. Your reasons may not be clear now, but they'll become readily apparent once you fully engage in something new. For those of you who feel you were born ready to surf, just get out there and get wet!

As you're doing your hair, controlling your jitters, and getting ready for your first "date" with surfing, we hope you're getting ready to begin a sport that you'll have a fruitful relationship with for years to come.

interview:

Dr. Liane Louie

Foundation officer, age thirty-nine
San Francisco, California

A former psychologist and beginner surfer, Liane reveals how surfing changed her life. Here, she gives us some sound advice on how to make that happen.

When was the first time you heard about surfing? When I actually went to Hawaii as a kid, I remember it was a part of life. I thought I would try it when I was seventeen, but I was really terrified. I was afraid I was going to drown. I'm not really a strong swimmer. I used to watch from the beach longingly.

Can you talk a little bit about surfing and the transition in your life? Actually, I began surfing right when I hit a major transition in my life. My boyfriend was diagnosed with cancer and that really made me reevaluate things. I realized that I needed to make things happen for myself. From that point I said, OK, I'm going to paddle [outrigger canoes]. I'm going to surf. I said to myself, OK, I want to do this, I have some fear. But what are the little baby steps I can do to make

this happen? You know, to me it's such a dream, to be on the water. . . . It just sounded awesome.

Is fear helpful? Yes, unless it's completely incapacitating. It's forced me to look at the truth and to take action, and to learn from my mistakes. If I've acted out of fear, I've learned a lot of lessons in overcoming fear. I'm proud of myself, that I took a little dream and made it happen. I thought, Before I die I'm gonna get up on a surfboard [laughter].

In overcoming your fears, was surfing the first thing you chose? Surfing wasn't the first thing I chose, but it was one of the first action steps. Two years ago, I reevaluated a lot of things. As I thought about things, I started making a list of things that I've always wanted

to do. Surfing was one of them. And as soon as I was ready to, I did it. Now I'm going to hike Half Dome [a rock formation in Yosemite National Park]. I'm going to rock climb. I even went fly-fishing! I've never done stuff like that! This change of life philosophy has totally changed me. I'm doing stuff I never thought I could do. Something snapped in me. The way I feel about life now is that I really have nothing to lose and everything to gain.

What advice do you have for women who want to try surfing? They should do it! I think they should face their fears. They should make a pros-and-cons list about what it is that is stopping them from doing it, and really look at that. If it's something that they really want to do, just do it. Come up with ways to try to make it happen. 'Cause

whether you're good at it or not, or if you get up on the board and you find out that you hate it, I don't think that's the point. The point is that you're doing something that you wanted to try. That's an accomplishment in and of itself. I think surfing is powerful. The connection with water is powerful—whether or not you actually get on a board or stay on a board. Just trying is huge. Just sitting on the water on the board, not even having gotten up, just looking around—I mean, that was a great feeling! I was connected to that dream. Whether or not I actually got up on the board, or whether or not I actually saw those dolphins. I know those are all blessings. Everything else is just icing on the cake. I was on the ocean and I was actually connected to my dream. And I think all women should feel that way.

CHAPTER 2

READY TO SURF

DIPPING A TOE IN

It's icy cold outside. Your bed is warm and the thought of plunging yourself into the realm of the fishes doesn't sound all that inviting. Yet there comes a time when you're ready, ready enough to dip a toe in.

you should be a decent swimmer in order to be a decent surfer

Talking to a good friend of ours about fear and surfing revealed something that keeps some women from dipping a toe in. As our conversation meandered this way and that, it became clear she wasn't so afraid of sharks or drowning or being hit in the head by a surfboard. She was more afraid of looking like a complete buffoon.

She had conquered the uncertainties of college, graduate school, the professional world, and the complexity of being a mommy. Now that she'd become competent in so many areas of her life, why would she try something totally new and difficult?

Surfing is difficult enough to make you feel like a beginner for years. Add to that the image of surfing as the ultimate in cool and you've got a recipe for embarrassment. Nobody wants to look unskilled or incompetent. In fact, there is even a term in surfing lingo for that unskilled, incompetent beginner: that person is called a *kook*. What a horrible word! Nevertheless, worry not. Remember that every single surfer was once a kook. (Believe it or not, after twenty years of surfing, we still worry occasionally about embarrassing ourselves in the water.) The problem is, if you spend all your time worrying about looking like a kook, you won't be able to listen calmly to your instructor or to paddle intentionally into that first wave.

Never fear, for in your hot little hands you've got a book. This book will help you answer all the questions you're too afraid to ask. The advice in these pages will help you decrease that time period of trial and error that comes along with being a kook. Of course, you'll learn from your mistakes—but here are some of the basics to get you out there.

BE A DECENT SWIMMER

How well do you need to swim before you can take a surf lesson? If you check the websites of a dozen different surf schools, you'll probably get a dozen different answers to that question.

Some say you only need to be able to swim with your head above water. Others say you should be able to swim 200 yards or wade for twenty minutes. The long and short of it is that at a surf lesson, there will be very little, if any, swimming going on. You will be wading out to your waist, standing in the water, and catching small whitewater waves. The swimming part comes into play if somehow a rip current pulls you out when you're not standing, or you paddle out to deeper water where your feet can't touch the sandy bottom. If for some reason this happens *and* you happen to lose the board that is leashed to your leg, you'll need to be a good enough swimmer to get back to shore.

Our advice: You should be a decent swimmer in order to be a decent surfer. If you want to be a good surfer, one who paddles out past the breakers, then eventually you should learn to be a "good" swimmer. A good swimmer can swim several laps in the pool with ease.

DO SOME SIT-UPS AND PUSH-UPS

You don't need to train for surfing the way you would train for an AIDS marathon. You should, however, build up enough strength so you can paddle and so you can push yourself up from a lying position to a standing position in one graceful motion. Doing sit-ups regularly will build up your core strength and give you more power in your paddling stroke. Doing push-ups will enable you to "pop" up to your feet without using your knees. For most experienced surfers, surfing regularly builds the appropriate muscles they need for surfing. However, if you can't find the time to be able to surf several times a week, we

A surf lesson with girlsAdventureOUT in Pacifica, CA.

Janine Daley showing us how to stay fit. Look for more exercises in Chapter 7.

recommend you read Chapter 7 so that you can condition your body for the rigors of surfing. Chapter 7 has more on surf fitness. As you advance, try some of the exercises in that chapter to improve your physical readiness for surfing.

SURFING SCHOOLS, SURFING BUDDIES, AND SURFING CLUBS

Surfing is essentially an individual sport. But if you want to improve steadily, it's enormously helpful to have someone to guide you. Surf schools are the best way to get started. They have all the equipment, know-how, and—for the most part—patient instructors to help you ease into surfing. The Appendix (see page 154) has some great tips on how to find a good surf school, followed by a list of women-centered schools.

Perhaps you've already had one lesson that helped you get started. But after the first lesson you're going to need someone to help you learn and remember the 101 tips you'll need in order to improve. One of the things that makes surfing so challenging compared to other sports is that the conditions are always changing. Each day you'll face different conditions. In fact, each wave will be different—and where you are in relation to that wave will drastically change what you're supposed to do at any given moment. For example, imagine trying to play tennis with a court that moves and undulates and a net that keeps changing places. Below we'll explore some ways to find guidance.

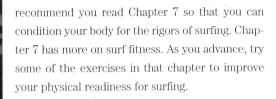

Your significant other

Isn't it great to have someone who loves you? If your partner in life also happens to be a surfer, wouldn't it be great to have the person who loves you teach you how to surf? Wrong. In most cases, this is actually a bad idea. Unless your partner is an excellent teacher and incredibly patient, we'd steer you away from getting lessons from your lover. We've seen many a quarrel on the beach or on the way home in the car when partners try to become teachers.

Imagine struggling against the elements—salt water in your nose, wave after wave slapping you in the face. Then imagine your loved one saying, "Dude, just get up! Why didn't you stand up? All you gotta do is just get up!" Unless they've taught surfing before, most surfers have conveniently forgotten the years and months of miserable trial and error they went through in order to become a competent surfer. They also seem to forget the hundreds of tiny things they do in order to surf well. Surfing becomes second nature—and you soon forget that you place your left hand next to your hip and your right hand next to your shoulder when you're standing up.

The details of surfing are what make it possible. To remember all these details and to be able to teach them in a calm and encouraging way is a rare attribute. This is why women's surf schools are so great. You'll be around a whole group of beginners and they'll be hooting and hollering every time you stand up or catch a wave. That's

you'll be around a whole group of beginners
and they'll be hooting and hollering

Tais Kintgen of Itacaré, Brazil. This woman can surf twenty-foot waves *and* change a diaper.

the kind of atmosphere you need when you're learning something new.

You might also be trying to "perform" in front of your significant other, and that adds an extra level of nervousness you just don't need when you're trying to learn how to walk on water. That being said, if your partner has the traits of a cheerleader, coach, and an excellent teacher, then your partner could be an invaluable resource. You're going to need as many resources as possible at your disposal for the months of wipeouts you're about to face.

A surfing buddy

Buddies are great. You don't have to sleep in the same bed with them after you've had a tiff. Finding a surf buddy is a great way to get yourself out there regularly to practice your surfing. On cold mornings when you're feeling the bliss of those 300-threadcount sheets on your body, a good surf buddy is great for tapping on your window to get you out of bed and out to the beach. You can find a buddy by talking to folks in your surf lesson, at a surf shop, or even online at websites like www. craigslist.org. Some websites have areas for "activity partners" where you can post your desire to find a surfing buddy in your area. You'll find more resources in the back of this book (see the list on page 162).

Surfing clubs

Most surfing clubs consist of older, experienced members who come together for camaraderie, to hold little contests, and to organize beach clean-up days. These clubs are not always a great place to learn because they tend to be geared toward people who already surf. Women's and novice surf clubs, however, are a new trend. These are a great way to get support and build a community of people who are learning how to surf. Try searching for these clubs or groups online at www.groups.yahoo.com or on a search engine. Women's surf clubs tend to have more beginners than other surf clubs, and they can be a supportive place for learners.

QUESTIONS YOU'RE TOO EMBARRASSED TO ASK

What do I need to bring to the beach?

Less is more when it comes to surfing. Here are the basics:

- a large towel for changing in and out of your wetsuit;
- your swimsuit (although most guys wear nothing under their wetsuit);
- if you're in an area with cold water (anything under 68° Fahrenheit), you'll need a wetsuit that fits;
- if you're in an area with warm water, long board-shorts will prevent chafing on your thighs;
- a rash guard (optional)—a really thin, stretchy, Lycra turtleneck shirt that some wear under their

> Women's surf clubs tend to have more beginners than other surf clubs

wetsuit to prevent chafing on their neck and arms. You could also wear a rash guard in warm water, without a wetsuit. There are thicker rash guards that can provide another layer of warmth;
- sunscreen (at least 15 SPF);
- your surfboard with leash attached;
- surf wax, unless you're learning on one of those foam or Softops boards that do not need wax. Here's a simple test: If you tap the top of the board with your knuckles and you hear a "knock," you've probably got a board that is meant to be waxed. There are different types of wax for different water temperatures (warm, cool, and cold). There's also a kind of wax called *base coat*. This is the type of wax you use on a new board, underneath a layer of regular wax.

What kind of board should I learn on?

We know you've seen television or magazine ads with people holding these pointy shortboards. Although they may look cool, these are NOT good boards to learn on. If you've signed up for a surf lesson, you're most likely going to be using a foam or Softops board. These boards are softer than fiberglass or epoxy; they do not need to be waxed; they have plastic fins; and they are longer, wider, and more stable than most boards.

you don't have to look like Gidget or Kate Bosworth to be a surfer

We know your friend might have an old spider-web-covered shortboard in their garage for you. But if you want to learn and have fun, we highly recommend you start on one of these beginner boards.

Can women of any size do this?

Contrary to popular belief, you don't have to look like Gidget or Kate Bosworth (from the movie *Blue Crush*) to be a surfer. As long as you can do a few push-ups and get up to your feet from a lying-down position, you can surf. Very large women surf, very skinny women surf, and even senior citizens are out there on boards. You'll need a board that floats you well and enough arm strength to paddle yourself forward.

What can I expect when renting a surf-board and wetsuit?

You can rent a wetsuit and surfboard at most surf shops. They'll have wetsuit sizes to fit most everyone, from XS to XXL. Wetsuits come in different thicknesses depending on how cold the water is. For example, a 4/3 wetsuit has a 4mm-thick body with 3mm-thick arms. Most shops charge by the day or by the hour. You can expect to pay between $10 to $25 a day for a wetsuit and about $15 to $30 a day for a surfboard. Most shops rent out foam or Softops longboards. When you're at the shop, try the wetsuit on to make sure it fits. If you don't already know, ask the shop to recommend a good spot for beginners. They'll know all the local spots and will try to recommend a place that has friendlier waves and friendlier people.

How cold will the water be?

Well, it all depends on where you're surfing and during what time of the year. If you're on the Big Island of Hawaii or in Bahia, Brazil, the water might be 68°F to 75°F, and there will be no need for a wetsuit. If you're surfing in Santa Cruz, California, or in New Jersey, the water might be 50°F to 60°F and it'll be as cold as hell without heat—so you'll definitely need a full wetsuit. Women tend to lose body heat more rapidly than men, so it may be a good idea to wear a thicker rash guard, a neoprene "hoodie" (a cap made out of wetsuit material), neoprene booties, and/or gloves.

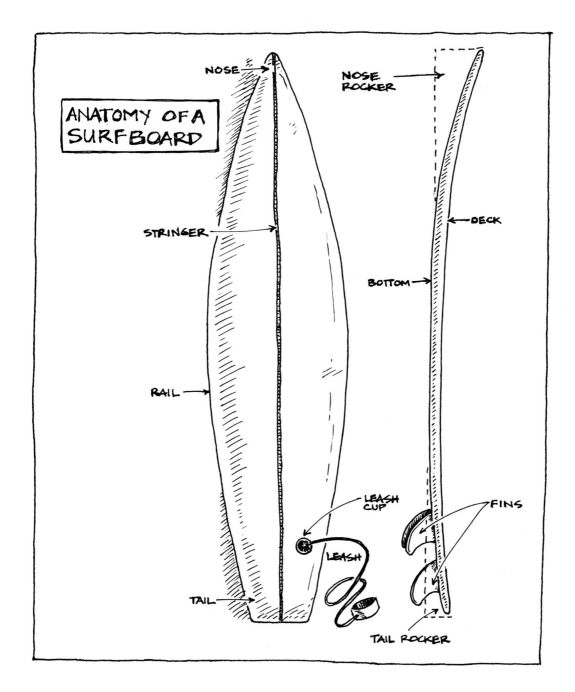

ANATOMY OF A SURFBOARD

NOSE

STRINGER

RAIL

TAIL

LEASH CUP

LEASH

NOSE ROCKER

DECK

BOTTOM

FINS

TAIL ROCKER

How do I get that big surfboard to the beach?

There are three basic ways to get a longboard to the beach:

1. Strap it to a hard roof rack. If you've got two bars going across the top of your car, you can strap your surfboard to the roof and ride in style. The bars should have thick foam pads on them. You'll also need some cinch straps or bungee cords to strap the board down. Wrap the leash around the board securely and then place

it's designed to keep a thin layer of water between the suit and your body

   the board (fins forward and facing up) on the foam pads and strap it down.
2. Strap it to a soft surf rack. If you don't have a roof rack, a cheaper way to go is to buy a soft surf rack at a surf shop for about fifty bucks. It consists of wide straps with foam pads on them. The instructions should be helpful.
3. Lay the board in the back of a truck. Make sure you put a towel underneath it and use bungee cords to keep the board from sliding around.

How do I put a wetsuit on?

Wetsuits are both a blessing and a curse. On the one hand, we wouldn't be able to surf in cold places without them. On the other hand, they can be incredibly frustrating to put on and take off. No matter how expensive they are, they do limit your movement. However, they do make you look slim and dangerous! Here's how to put one on:

1. Do it in the beach parking lot (or at a surf shop, if you are trying one on). Putting on your wetsuit at home is not a good idea. By the time you get to the water, you'll be sweating and itchy. Some women like to wear their swimsuits underneath but others feel that the suit can bunch up. Try both and see how you're most comfortable.
2. Take the dry wetsuit and make sure it's not inside out. (The seams of a wetsuit are more apparent on the inside than they are on outside.)
3. Unzip the zipper and slide your toe into one of the legs of the suit. Make sure the zipper will end up being in the back. Once your toe is in, pull (careful; long fingernails can rip a suit) the suit over your heel. Repeat with your other foot.
4. Pull the suit up your legs and up to your waist. Pull the suit in places where it's bunched up. If you have a rash guard, make sure it's on.
5. If you don't have someone to watch your stuff, you'll have to put your car key in your wetsuit and lock everything else in the car. Most wetsuits have a secure key pocket next to the zipper. Put the key in the pocket and slide your arms into the wetsuit. Don't worry; in all these years, we've never lost a key this way
6. If you've got long hair, put it up. Grab the long strap connected to the zipper, arch your back,

and pull the strap upward (like pulling an arrow out of your quiver) until it won't go any farther.

7. While holding the strap/zipper up, grab the Velcro piece on the neck of the wetsuit and fasten it over the zipper.

Yes, it's supposed to be tight and form-fitting. You'll know the wetsuit's too tight only if it's too short to cover your wrists and ankles or if it's *really* difficult to zip up or move in. Also, the basic idea to remember about a wetsuit is that it does not keep you dry. It's designed to keep a thin layer of water between the suit and your body. Your body warms up this thin layer, thereby insulating you from the cold. Now, you look like a surfer!

Is it safe to surf in areas that have sharks when you have your period?

This is a good and surprisingly common question for women who surf. While surfing can be very good for women dealing with cramps (it engages the stomach muscles), it is totally understandable that women surfers with their period would be concerned about attracting sharks. Most areas of the world do not have dangerous sharks; however, for those select few areas that do, there are conflicting opinions about this issue. Most professional women surfers don't let their period get in the way of their surfing. Shark expert Ralph S. Collier from the Shark Research Committee (a tax-exempt nonprofit scientific research organization) had this to say about the issue:

"There is no scientific data that confirms human blood to be an attractant to sharks. A number of years ago, friend and colleague H. David Baldridge conducted a number of experiments using human body fluids to determine whether they were potentially provocative to sharks. One of the fluids tested was human blood. The results in these specific tests showed that human blood did not attract sharks. However, there are other fluids that are also associated with humans and female menstrual cycles. Without any positive determination, sometimes 'it is better to be safe than sorry.' My personal suggestions have always been to avoid water contact during that time of the month, even though there is no scientific evidence to support this suggestion."

OK, I'm at the beach. I've got my wetsuit on, my car key tucked away, and my surfboard. What do I do now?!

We remember what it was like being at the beach parking lot, hoping that we'd do everything "right" so no one would find out we were beginners. Here are some basic steps:

1. **Wax that board.** Unless you're learning on a foam or Softtops board, you'll need to wax your surfboard. Please be aware: you wax a surfboard for the opposite reason you wax skis. Skis are waxed on the bottom so that they will slide more easily across the snow. Surfboards are waxed on the top so that you *won't* slide off the

board. Place the board, with fins down, onto the sand. If the board has never been waxed before, start by rubbing on a layer of base-coat wax. Once you've done that, wax the board gently in small circular motions from the tail of the board to about three-quarters of the way to the tip. The idea is to gently build up little bumps of wax that will allow your feet to grip onto the board when you're riding.

2. **Carry the board to the beach**. Carrying a board is actually not as easy as it looks. First, make sure that the leash is wrapped around the board and Velcro-fastened to itself. Nothing looks sillier than a surfer who's dragging her leash through the sand as she's walking to the beach. The preferred way to hold the board is under your arm

as a beginner, you'll be catching whitewater (waves that have already broken)

with the board flat against your side. However, with most longboards, you've got to have pretty long arms to do that. Some people opt for the classic "board on the head" technique of a bygone era. This seems to work well for most women, as long as you can balance the board on your head while steadying it with one hand.

3. **Sit on the beach and look for a good spot.** Looking for the right spot to paddle out from is a time-honored ritual passed down from generations of soul surfers to grommets (young surfers) worldwide. You see them on foggy mornings on every coast, with hooded sweatshirts, those big fuzzy Ugg™ boots, and a cup of java in hand. They are pointing and talking, psyching themselves up for the impending session, trying to find a spot that has the best form and the fewest people. Sit on the beach and look at what the ocean is doing and what other surfers are doing. At this point, choosing the right spot for a beginner is a bit like a novice choosing a good wine: it's hard to choose because they don't seem *that* different. As a beginner, you'll be catching whitewater (waves that have already broken). Once a wave has broken there is not much difference in their form, so you don't need to worry much about what section of the beach has the best form for you. What you should consider is rip tides and crowds.

A riptide, or a channel, is a section of the beach where water collects and gets drawn out toward the ocean or toward one end of the beach or the other. You'll know you're in a "rip" area because you'll be battling a constant undertow. It's generally tiring and can sometimes be dangerous. As you're searching for a good spot, look to see if there's an area where the water's quickly moving outward like a river and try to avoid that spot. If you find yourself in the water in a rip area, make sure your feet are planted in sand below and walk your way back to shore. If you can't go back to shore, paddle along the shoreline to cut off the rip current and then head into shore. A rip current is usually only on one part of the beach.

The last thing to consider when finding a good spot is staying out of the way of other surfers. Surfers tend to get upset when they've been working hard to catch the right wave and just as they make it to the right section of a wave to pull off a fancy maneuver, they find an unsuspecting surfer with a terrified look standing right in their way. Try to find an area where you're not right behind a gaggle of surfers (surfers generally face the ocean). If the surfers are pretty far out, they'll probably pull out of the wave before it reaches you.

4. **Put on your leash.** Walk to the water's edge and take a deep breath. Remember, this is all about having fun! Before you get into the water, you have to figure out whether you're a goofy-foot or a regular-foot. On a skateboard or snowboard, do you naturally ride with your right foot forward or your left foot forward? If you don't have a skateboard, try this: Stand with your legs together and have someone push you backwards. Whichever leg goes back first will be your back leg. Or, try lying down, pretend

you're paddling a surfboard, then try popping up to your feet (with feet pointing to the left side of the board or to the right). Pop up, bend your knees, and throw your arms out. Which foot naturally goes to the front and which one

try to find an area where you're not right behind a gaggle of surfers

goes to the back? If you ride with your right foot forward, you're a goofy-foot, and the leash goes on your left foot (the foot that will be toward the back of the surfboard when you stand up). If you ride with your left foot forward, you're a regular-foot, and everything is vice versa. (See illustration on page 25.)

Please note that leashes are to be used as a last resort if you absolutely cannot hang on to your board. Letting your board go is not generally a good idea, unless you absolutely have to. If you must let the board go, remember that your board can be tossed in the area around you up to a twenty-foot diameter. Make sure there are no other surfers around.

5. **Wade into the water up to your belly.** Carry your board into the water; when you've gotten in as deep as your thighs, put the board in the

water (fins facing down). Hold the floating board with two hands along the edges, with the nose of the board facing forward (perpendicular to the beach). If you let the board go horizontal to the beach, when a wave comes it will flip the board sideways and could bounce up and knock you in the face. Always have the board held, floating by your side. As a wave comes, walk out toward the wave, grab the board, bend your knees, lift the board up (nose slightly higher than the tail), and jump the board over the whitewater. As soon as you can, stand up in the sand and get ready for the next one. Do this little routine for a while, until you get used to the feeling of holding the board properly and jumping over the waves. The idea here is to get out far enough so you can catch whitewater that is strong enough to propel you and your surfboard toward the beach.

Will I stand up my first time? If I don't, does that mean I'm no good at this?

Let's just say that it takes many people months to learn how to stand up on a surfboard. On the other hand, some folks stand up the first time. This is not a competition. Surfing is not the easiest sport to learn—and it's even more difficult to master. A woman we met on the beach told us she had been a skier and snowboarder for many years. She even had the world record for tandem hangliding! She said surfing was the hardest thing she'd ever tried to master. On a ski hill or a soccer field, the mountain or the field is pretty static. In the water, however, you've got all these waves and tides going this way and that. The whole thing feels pretty chaotic.

As you start to understand how waves work, you'll start to get a feeling about where you need to be and what you need to be doing at any particular time. Having said this, standing up is quite a distance from mastering the sport. With good instruction, it's very possible that you'll stand up your first time surfing. It will be an indescribable rush. In fact, just lying on the board and being moved by a wave is a fantastic rush. If you don't stand up your first time, don't worry. You can join us—and thousands of other men and women like us—who decided to keep trying. Whatever you do, make absolutely sure that you do one thing incredibly well. That one thing is to enjoy yourself immensely.

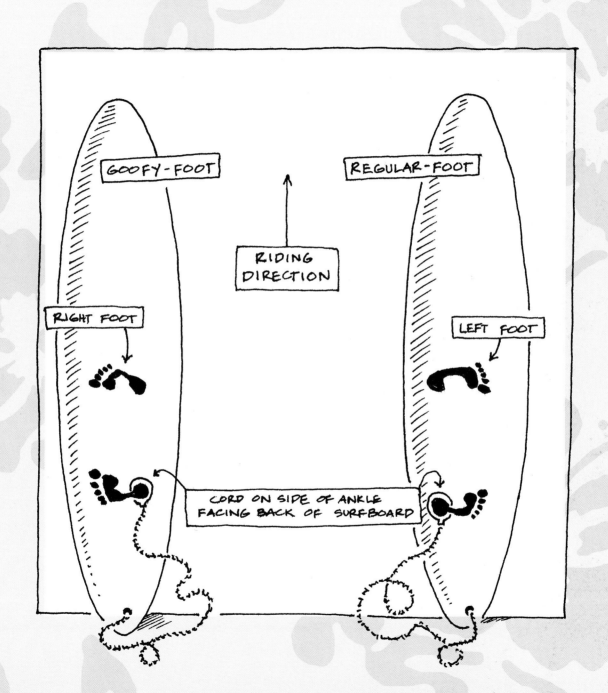

interview

Yasmeen Mussard-Afcari

Third grader, age eight
Berkeley, California

An eight-year-old's view of the world can be so refreshing. Here, in her own words, Yasmeen talks about her first experiences with surfing, and provides some sound advice to us older girls.

How do you feel about the ocean? I feel like I was born there. I love swimming in it. It's so cool. I don't know, it just makes me feel better. It soothes me.

Do you have any fear of the ocean? Um, a slight one.

What do you do when you have that fear? I just try to think about something else.

When you see surfers out in the water, what do you think? I think, like, Wow. I want to do that too. I want to do that by myself too. I've been surfing seven times now. Sometimes it's freezing. The water is really cold. There were no good waves today but it was really cool. It wasn't scary today because I was wearing a floaty-thing and my dad picked me up right away when I fell in. There wasn't, like, time for me to get scared.

What advice would you have for other girls who want to surf? Um, I don't know; just don't be afraid. Because that's your weakness, if you're afraid of the water. You gotta turn that weakness into, like, power. I just think about how proud everybody's gonna be and how proud I'm gonna be if I accomplish what I'm doing. But I think next time, and the first time you surf, that you should try doing the starfish [a swim-lesson method for floating]. Don't give up on your first try. I wanted to go in at first because the waves were so big.

What advice do you have for parents who want to teach their kids to surf? I don't think that they should push them so hard. You know, like, the more the parents push the kids, the more the kids get afraid. They have to go at their own pace, not at the grown-up's pace.

What about people who say that surfing is for boys? They are totally wrong. If they haven't noticed, there are so many crews of women surfing, like *Blue Crush*, and like what you see on the beach. There's lots of women surfing. Women are very, very strong.

Anything else you want to say about surfing? It rocks!

CHAPTER 3

GETTING OUT THERE

Friend, we want you in the water. But before you get out there, there are a few things you should know. Women-centered surf schools are a great way to learn the basics—and a great way to make your first efforts pleasurable. You'll find a list of women-centered schools, and suggestions on how to evaluate a school, in the back of this book (see Appendix II). If you can't find a school near you, or if you're the kind of person who wants some knowledge before you go for a lesson, we've broken down a few of the practical and cultural fac-

using a beginner's board will make your entry into surfing much more pleasant

tors that will help you navigate your way into surfing. Empowered with this knowledge, you'll be less likely to give up when the going gets tough.

YOUR INNER GIRL

If you consider yourself somewhat grown-up, read on. Think back, to your younger days. These were the days when pigtails were the hairstyle of choice, when you could play for hours in the sand, and when boys were mostly just a nuisance. If you're lucky, perhaps things haven't changed much for you since those days. For most of us, they've changed quite a bit. These days, you might be spending more time at work, in traffic, or in line than you are playing in the sand.

Yet in order for you to get the most you can out of surfing, you're going to need some of that incredibly powerful girl-energy. That's the kind of energy you called upon when you were squealing in delight as you ran in and out of the waves. It's the kind of energy you'd use to stomp on the local bully's toe and then run into the girl's bathroom. Girl-energy is wild and sparkling and deeply committed to fun.

When you go out for your first surf lesson, you may be a bit afraid. There will be someone giving you instructions. You'll be concentrating, you'll be very serious about *doing it right*. This worry about doing it right will get in your way. If you feel the seriousness coming on, take a deep breath and remember your pigtails. This is all about fun, right?

CHOOSING YOUR BOARD

Which board is right for you? Most surf shops will start you out on a foam or Softops board. This is a good idea, because these boards are really stable, and soft enough so that getting hit by one will not cause major injury. Using a beginner's board will make your entry into surfing *much* more pleasant. Remember, in the early stages, we're trying to build the evidence of success. Don't try to be a hero by starting off on a six-foot-three shortboard!

But as you progress—as you begin to stand up on waves confidently and regularly, after the surfing bug has bit you—you'll be standing at a surf shop, arms folded, looking at this endless row of boards. You'll be forced to make a decision on what kind of board you'd like to buy. Be aware: your choice in boards can have a real impact on how you enter the sport. There are two types of surfboards and therefore two types of surfers: longboarders and shortboarders. A culture has developed around each of these boards—a particular surfing style, with its own aesthetic and cultural norms.

Just for the record, we are both primarily longboarders, so we're somewhat biased toward those who choose longer sticks for their quiver. (Note: Your collection of surfboards is called your quiver. Isn't that cool?)

The longboard has a direct connection to ancient Hawaiian surfboards made of deliciously complex caramel Hawaiian Koa wood. It is considered the board of choice for soul surfers. Longboards run approximately eight to ten feet or so,

Remember those big grins you had as a girl? Two surf buddies take off on a southern California wave.

Two Brazilian surfistas smile after a great session.

and are oblong shaped with one fin or three. Long-boards are the cruisers of the surfing world, and are generally ridden by those who value grace over pushing the physicality of the sport. For longboard-ers, it's all about grace, grace, grace. The footwork, the flow. You see these men and women, standing gracefully erect and totally in control. They ride as if they're walking on water, as if they're doing the Argentine Tango—making the board dance while caressing the lines of a wave like a lover backed by Al Green and his angelic backup singers. Although a lot of younger people are riding longboards these days, these boards are generally associated with more seasoned surfriders.

Shortboarding, on the other hand, has a differ-ent aesthetic, and therefore a different measure of proficiency. Shortboarders value quick turns, snaps, and aerial attacks versus the mellow turns of the longboarder. Shortboards are the Ferraris of the surfing set. They are incredibly quick, maneuverable, and responsive. Shortboarders do things that longboarders could never dream of doing. They can actually fly in the air with their boards and do 360s. So shortboarding is almost a different sport than longboarding, and, in many places, it has its own subculture built around it.

In competitive surfing, longboarding and shortboarding are judged completely separately. It's strange, you know. How do you judge something like surfing? There are no goals to be scored and no home runs to be hit. There is no clear measure that would allow you to unmistakably define one surfer as the winner and the other as not the winner. It becomes, then, much more about style—a marriage of art and sport. Surfers are judged on what kind of a line they paint on the canvas of the waves. Despite these distinctions, there are plenty of shortboarders who consider themselves soul surfers, and the lines are blurring all the time.

Once, when we were out in the water on the Big Island in Hawaii, we asked some Hawaiian surfers about longboarding versus shortboarding. They were rather perplexed. They didn't identify themselves as one or the other. They were much more connected to the ocean and its conditions. "It all depends on the wave, brah," they said. "If it's steep and fast we pull out our shortboards. If it's peeling and slow we take out our longboards."

We should also mention that there is a third general category of surfboard called the big-wave gun. How's that for testosterone? A gun is a very long, very pointy, skinny board designed for catching the biggest of waves. Its narrowness and length give it incredible speed when you're paddling, so you can drop in on the face of those twenty-foot-plus waves. There's also a variation of this board called a tow-board. Tow-boards are somewhat shorter (with foot straps attached to the deck of the board) and are designed for being towed by a jet-ski into the world's largest waves. These types of boards and the surfing that goes with them are for a handful of people around the world with questionable sanity. For us regular surfers, our choices are pretty much limited to using longboards, shortboards, or something in between.

you see these men and women, standing gracefully erect and totally in control

When considering your choice between longboards versus shortboards, a beginner should start on a longboard, because of the added stability. Once you're comfortable with that, you can try shortboarding and see how you like it. There's even a board that's in between a shortboard and a longboard, called an *egg*. Then it becomes a question of style. Do you want to explore your radical self or your graceful Zen self? Your identity as a surfer is yours to choose.

CHOOSING YOUR SPOT

How can you get out there on the waves without impinging on someone else's turf? As we've mentioned before, there are different cultural norms for longboarders versus shortboarders. You'll also find that different surf spots have their own culture—and these may vary greatly. In order to have a good experience, it's important that you choose a spot where it will be easier to learn how to surf. Your decision will have as much to do with the waves at that particular spot as with the people who surf there.

For example, we've noticed quite a few different scenes up and down the California coast. The first thing we try to gauge is the level of *localism*. What is localism? Localism essentially describes how territorial surfers are about their surf spots. Some surfers who've lived and surfed in a particular area for a long time feel possessive about their local break. This phenomenon sometimes results in unfriendliness in the water, locals taking your waves, and sometimes (though rarely), violence in the water.

two different spots
can have two totally
different surf cultures

So in some places, surfing becomes a question of turf. How can we get you out there on the waves without impinging on somebody's turf? To get a sense of how different each beach can be with respect to beginners, we'll start by looking at the difference between two California surf spots.

Two different spots can have two totally different surf cultures. Let's compare Encinitas and Santa Cruz. In Encinitas, there's like a hundred places to surf within a stretch of coast ten miles long. The waves you encounter within these ten miles tend to be mellow, laid-back, peeling waves. So as a result, you have mellow, laid-back, peeling surfers out there generally sharing the bounty of plentiful waves for all. And because there are plenty of waves, there's plenty of time for conversation and banter. People talk about their kids getting braces, their latest trip down to Baja, or the newest addition to their quiver.

Surfers in Encinitas are known to have gone to a particular surf break—the same spot in the lineup—for twenty years. So it's like a second job for these men and women (you wonder if they actually do have jobs outside of surfing). Have you ever seen that cartoon where an old confident sheepdog and a conniving coyote come to work every day with their metal lunchboxes, punch in on the time clock, and then begin their battle of stealing or protecting sheep? Some surfers come to the same spot every day and clock in like it's a job. Even though they are in competition for the same waves, there is this feeling of communion, of understood fellowship. And we all feel welcome.

Santa Cruz, on the other hand, has about twelve spots along a coastal stretch of ten miles

Newbies at Las Olas Surf Safaris in Mexico look for a suitable spot to paddle out.

The joy of standing up on a wave is indescribable.

and has about a million surfers who are trying to catch the same waves. The waves in Santa Cruz can be gnarly. "Bowling Nuggets!" we used to call them, as we'd drive up over the ridge. These waves are mostly reef breaks, whose steep, pitching waves are generally unforgiving. Gnarly waves—coupled with the fact that it's as cold as a penguin's nuts in iced tea—makes for quite a high-stakes scene out in the water. We have this theory that cold places have more uptight, unfriendly people. Anyhow, the problem is too many surfers, not enough waves. This is a recipe for disaster and we've actually seen a few fights over waves.

It's also good to remember that a mean surfer who just yelled at you might be doing you a favor by keeping you out of a spot not suited for learning. It can be dangerous to surf around beginners, so sometimes the locals are simply doing the job of keeping people safe.

However, in just about every surf town you can find beginner breaks (even in Santa Cruz) where the waves are more gentle and there are a greater number of learners out in the water. These breaks have more mellow and forgiving waves and more mellow and forgiving surfers. To find a good beginner break, just go down to the local surf shop and ask. Most surfers are happy to show you those breaks because the waves tend to be smaller there. Asking this question is the equivalent of asking where the "bunny" (beginner) hill is at a ski resort. By asking, you're also showing your respect for the safety of other surfers.

In the movie *Step Into Liquid*, by Dana Brown, we see the lengths surfers go to find waves—from surfing Lake Michigan, to riding the waves caused by supertanker ships along the coast of Texas. Surfers also have their "secret spots," where they escape to for crowd-free surfing. These are highly guarded commodities—and if we told you about them, we might be kicked out of this club. Nonetheless, you should talk to surfers in parking lots and on windswept ridges. Trust good surf schools. They'll tell you which spots are good for beginners. When we were in San Diego recently

in just about every surf town you can find beginner breaks

we discovered a spot frequented by an unusually high number of women. Somehow this spot had developed into a welcoming place for women. When you find a good spot, you'll know it—and you'll begin to understand the wave and, more importantly, the culture of that particular place.

CHOOSING YOUR WAVE

Waves break when the combination of water, wind, the moon's gravity (tides), and the shape of the land come together in perfect harmony. They are perpetual—a constant flow of energy, lapping on seaweed-strewn shores all over our little planet.

They are created by swells in the ocean, caused by storms, earthquakes, and winds. They generally form in deep water and develop across miles of ocean to meet the sand at your local beach. So they've come a long way to meet you. Of the millions of waves that come, each one is different, lasting only for a few precious moments. You'll have to pick and choose which

waves break essentially because water follows the shape of the land

ones you want. And you'll have to decide if this one's for you or if you're going to let it pass you by.

Three Types of Breaks

Waves break essentially because water follows the shape of the land. When the surface of the ocean floor rises abruptly, it pushes the water upwards until gravity causes the lip of the wave to curl over and fall on itself.

Beach Break

At a beach break, sandbars in the ocean floor cause the moving water to push upwards and break. Beach breaks are usually the safest breaks because the sandy bottom makes for a soft landing on wipeouts, and because the waves are generally not as steep as reef breaks.

Reef Break

A reef break works on the same premise as a beach break, except that the ocean bottom has reefs or rocks that cause water to surge upwards, forming a breaking wave. Reef breaks move from flat water to a breaking wave fairly quickly. They are generally steeper waves that require the surfer to get up to her feet quickly. There is also a higher risk of cuts and scrapes when wipeouts occur.

Point Break

A point break forms waves in a different way. If you look at a point break from the sky (as in the illustration on page 40), you'll see that point breaks form because oncoming water is pushed up as it hits a piece of land that is jutting out from the rest of the coastline. The "point," or the part of the land that juts out the farthest, pushes the surging water upwards and causes the wave to break in one direction (i.e., from left to right, or vice versa). Point breaks form waves in a very predictable area. Surfers have an easy paddle out to these waves and line up as close to the point as possible to catch the breaking waves.

There are generally two parts of the wave: the part that has broken and the part that is yet to

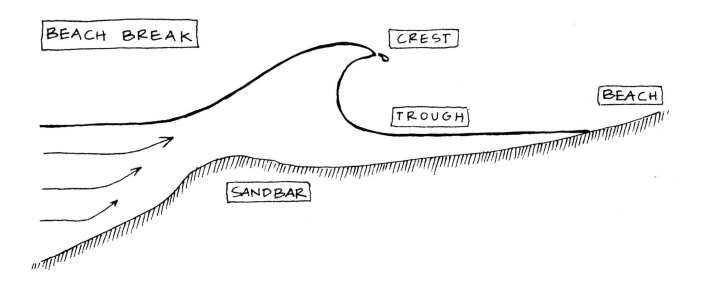

BEACH BREAK

CREST

TROUGH

BEACH

SANDBAR

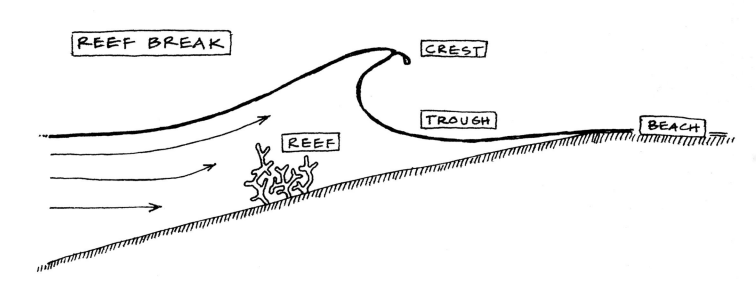

REEF BREAK

CREST

TROUGH

BEACH

REEF

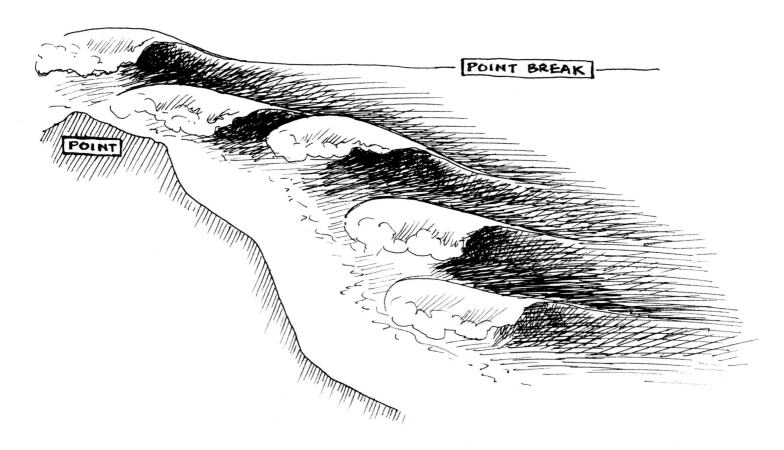

POINT BREAK

POINT

break. When you are starting out, you'll be catching whitewater—waves that have already broken. Why? Because we want to get you going with the rush of being pushed by water without the fear of "going over the falls." Going over the falls is when you find yourself at the steepest part of the wave (the lip) and then it throws you over the falls and into the whitewater. Unless you have a lot of experience, your board might pearl (that is, nose-dive), and then you'll be pushed down into the soup. This is not a good thing, because your whole body will feel squashed and tumbled and there will be sand stuck in your teeth. However, if we start you out catching whitewater, there will be an initial

rush, a bit of chaotic bumpiness while you're in the whitewater, and then you'll be pushed ahead where it's a bit calmer. Your board will stabilize and then you can pop up to your feet in one incredibly graceful motion.

So the first wave you choose will be whitewater—and in that case, any whitewater will do. When you're "on the inside" and riding the whitewater, you'll have less of a chance of getting in the way of other surfers. Riding whitewater also gives you time to get used to the way waves break and to learn how to surf safely. As you progress, you'll begin to *earn* the respect of other surfers.

PARTS OF A WAVE

THE LIP

THE SHOULDER

THE POCKET

THE FALLS

THE WALL

THE BARREL OR TUBE

THE WHITEWATER

THE SOUP

interview:

Cheryl Larsen

Senior project manager, age forty-two ,
San Francisco, California

Cheryl's simultaneous deep fear and deep
love of the ocean is palpable. In this honest interview, we hear about her process
of dealing with fear and finding the bliss
of surfing. (You can read about Cheryl's
first surf lesson in Chapter 5.)

How do you feel about the ocean? I feel . . . Probably some of my most powerful emotions are around the ocean. It's expansive, it has space, it's beautiful, and it's very scary . . . for the same reason that it's beautiful. It's just a very powerful place to be.

Do you remember your first experience with the ocean? I do remember being young and large swells would come and we would let our bodies go up with the swell and it would pass through. It would raise us way in the air. It was like we were flying. That all changed for me when I had some traumatic experiences as an adolescent. The trauma and being in the ocean all got wrapped up together in my mind and then I just didn't go in the ocean anymore. Now when I go to the

water, and even if I feel it around my ankles, I get really scared.

How does the ocean relate to your life now? Well, I'm very much an observer of my life and I really want to be in it and living it. There's this fear that if I'm in it, what could come by? The ocean is really a metaphor for that. It's very symbolic: I'm on the beach and I can't get into it. And I want to so badly. I can't step into life. The ocean is life and I can't get into it. There's incredible power there. When we started talking about surfing it reignited everything. And I said, "You know, I want this." And I'm going to have to conquer it if I want to get there.

What is making you ready now? I want to be at the table and I want to be

participating. When you get down in the pit with your demons, that's the hardest time. I've worked so hard for so many years. But I'm learning to be gentle with myself. I feel it happening. My foundation is shifting. I deserve to be here. Just being really gentle and pleasant. I'm in it and I'm saying, you know, this is life.

When you hear the word "surfer," what comes to your mind? My first images are of boy groups. You know, it's kind of a boys' club. Women surfers I have a totally different feeling for. They're warriors to me. The guys are out there playing and doing their thing. But then I look at what they're actually doing . . . Wow. Women surfers are, like, commanding respect in a male world. It's changing now but it's still a male domain. The

ocean is not the domain of one gender or another; it is feminine and masculine.

So you're thinking about trying surfing. How do you feel about that? Oh, I'm not thinking about it, I'm GOING to try surfing. How I feel about it constantly changes, day to day almost—and is affected by hormones, stress at work, how much sleep I've had the night before. I just realized I'm going to have to suit up and do it.

What do you think you'd need to enter into the water? I'd need to know some basic information about how a wave works. But really, that's second-ary. It's really about being able to center myself, to know that I can trust myself and to trust the person I'm with. I think

that's really it. It's an exercise in letting go. It needs to happen.

When I say the words "Cheryl Larsen, Surfer," how does that feel? I shirk from that, because I can't see that right now. But that's part of the process. I'm a bit intimidated by that stereotype. You know, I don't want to be disrespected or ridiculed.

What kind of advice do you have for other women who might have some fear of the ocean? Well, not having fully conquered it, I don't know if I can give anything concrete. My path to it is: You need to be gentle with yourself. I can't go there unless I'm gentle, and trusting and accepting; unless I know who I am.

CHAPTER 4

OVERCOMING FEAR

SOME THOUGHTS ON FEAR

BY LIANE LOUIE AND KIA AFCARI

Fear is noise. It's that AM-radio static that blocks out the beautiful music. There is no denying it. It lives with us. And although we hate to quote tiny green wise men from *Star Wars* movies, Yoda did have some wisdom for us: "Much fear I sense in you, padwan learner. Fear leads to hate, hate leads to anger, anger leads to suffering . . ."

Yes, we all know that fear can be an obstacle in our lives. So what do we do? We try to squash it. We try to put it in a jar. We try to stuff it under our beds at night next to cobwebs and slippers, child-hood monsters, and forgotten dreams.

Fear is that moment, that golden microsecond, before you make or *don't* make that decision.

Fear is the judge; it's that I-can't voice from a million moments of doubt placed in your lap by naysayers and worrywarts.

Many surfers speak of how fear helped them through difficult situations. Fear can motivate or protect us. And although it can be helpful, fear as a limiting factor closes possibilities in your life. It keeps you from thinking straight. It makes you question your inherent capability. It prevents you from thinking freely and creatively. You can't be present when you are overrun by fear.

Part of the problem with fear is that we have fear, and then we berate ourselves for having it. In the United States, there's a cultural emphasis placed on "picking yourself up, and getting over it." Unfortunately, just denying you have fear is usually not enough to help you move past it.

> "All human actions are motivated at their deepest level by one of two emotions, fear or love." —Neale Donald Walsch

Surfers in Pacifica, California.

It's been said that courage is not the absence of fear, but rather the ability to act in spite of it. Every human being has fear. When Amelia Earhart set out on her transatlantic journey, fear was one of her passengers. She had to own it, analyze it, and ultimately move beyond it to do something that most thought impossible. When Rell Sunn, the queen of women's surfing, was faced with breast cancer, she had to push through fear for fifteen years in order to reclaim her life as a surfer, waterwoman, and inspirer. She refused to believe that her cancer or her fear could limit her.

For many of us, fear multiplies after each successful hesitation. Each time we let our fear limit us, fear jumps for joy, waving tiny flags in our hearts, constricting, squeezing, opening space for the other fear leeches that have been waiting to get in. Each time fear wins, we lose.

the idea is to sit and actually *feel* your fear, release some emotions around it

When we become fearful or anxious, both physiological and psychological symptoms manifest themselves. Physiological reactions to fear or stress include: tension in your muscles, shaking or tremors, difficulty with breathing or hyperventilation, increased heart rate and blood pressure, changes in blood circulation resulting in abdominal and intestinal discomfort, sweating, weakness, or dizziness. Psychological symptoms might include memory problems, black-and-white thinking, negative thinking, rumination, and self-blame.

AAAAAggh! I don't know about you, but all this talk about fear is driving me a little nuts. Let's breathe for a moment. Yes. Oxygen tends to assuage fear, like a confident postal carrier petting an angry pit bull. The dog begins to wag its tail a bit.

Yes, fear exists. And if it exists, what the hell do we do about it? It seems to me that we either carry it like a backpack of bricks, or, as a dear female friend would say, "We snatch it like a spear and use it to hunt our prey." This friend, by the way, ran a triathlon—despite the fact that she didn't know how to swim, bike, or run. She surmounted a physical fear and then went on to overcome her fear of success. After years of searching for a viable career, she's now studying hard in law school. Like the women in this book, she's learned that conquering fear sets the stage for further conquests.

So how do we turn fear into a spear? How do we acknowledge it, grab it, and then turn it into joy, success, or an epic tube ride on a beautiful wave? Here are three methods for working with fear.

Go to the past and reevaluate the present

Let's start with acknowledgment. Reevaluation counseling is one way to acknowledge and address your fears. Here's a brief example of how reevaluation counseling works.

Get a trusted friend who listens well to sit in front of you and listen intently. Tell her you want to try something and that it may feel strange, but that you need her full attention *without* advice. The idea is to sit and actually *feel* your fear, release some emotions around it, and then—over the course of many sessions—reevaluate your current situation with a clearer mind.

Try saying the following to your friend, five times slowly: "I'm scared about _____ (fill in the blank)." OK. Now breathe ten times slowly.

Now try saying this five times slowly: "Being scared makes me feel _____, and I don't want to feel _____."

Now this: "The first time in my memory that I felt scared about something like _____ was _____. I remember feeling so _____."

Now this: "Today is a totally different day, and I'm a totally different person. Even though I'm scared about _____, I can choose to do something about it anyway."

OK. Now the noise of fear might still be there. Nonetheless, did you experience any deep yawns, any goose bumps, tears, sweating, jitters, or shakes? If you did, this is your body releasing some of that fear. Sometimes things happen to us and we bottle those feelings up because we've gotten the message that it's not OK to cry.

Imagine a young girl who falls and scrapes her knee and then is told to just brush it off and keep going. Her feelings get squashed and stored in her consciousness. As she grows, these feelings leak out whenever she gets close to a bicycle. Although as an older person, her fear of riding bicycles is mostly irrational, her mind replays the feelings that are "stuck" in her consciousness. Going back to that moment and releasing the emotion could allow her to reevaluate her current situation and overcome her fear of riding bikes.

Use cognitive coping strategies

Another way to deal with fear is by using cognitive coping strategies. First, begin by dissecting your negative thoughts from everyday experiences. For example, while you're getting in the water you might be thinking, "Oh no, what if I fall? What if I drown? I'm no good at this . . ." In fact, all that is really happening is that you are getting in the water. You can begin to monitor your thoughts, especially your negative ones, in relation to particular situations. You can keep a journal or a log. In this way, you gather some evidence of your negative thinking.

Try using logical comebacks in response to your negative thinking. Logical comebacks are reasonable, balanced ways of testing your hypotheses and putting your automatic thoughts to the test. For example, challenge your assumption that "I'm going to drown" by assuring yourself that you're a competent swimmer and you've never even come close say something totally different, such as: "Oh my God, the waves are so big; what do I do? I'll stay on the beach. I'm not a good swimmer. It's cold. What about sharks? What if I die? Do I have a heart condition? But I should be brave; it's not good to be scared. *What will people think of me?*"

Fear and intelligent concern are two different things. Fear has all that noise and self-doubt wrapped up in it. Intelligent concern comes from a

as you begin to tackle your fears, monitor your feelings and take small steps to achieve your goals

to drowning. In this way, you are challenging your assumption with rational thoughts. What modifications can you make to these beliefs to make your outlook more balanced? You might ask yourself, "What evidence do I have to refute this belief? What evidence do I have to support it?"

Some might say that fear is helpful, for it protects you from harm. We think intelligent concern is helpful—and that is something quite different from fear. An example of intelligent concern is telling yourself: "OK, the waves are very big today; I'll just go waist-deep so that I can paddle for whitewater." Fear might lead you to

calm place. Fear comes from a frantic place. Intelligent concern is fear stripped of all the noise.

All that noise gets in the way of thinking clearly. It gets in the way of listening well. It blocks you from being fully present, confident, and aware of each moment. Have you ever had someone try to teach you something but you were too worried about not doing well and you couldn't take it all in? The fear of failure and past hurts blocks us from being in the present moment.

Take small steps

As you begin to tackle your fears, monitor your feelings and take small steps to achieve your goals. As you approach the ocean, take note of how you're feeling. Are your hands sweaty, shaking? Is

your heart pounding? Are you breathing faster? On a scale of one to ten—with one feeling very calm and ten feeling very anxious—how would you rate your feelings now?

Write down the different steps you could take to achieve your goals. For example: step one, take swimming lessons; step two, wade in the water regularly and take surfing lessons, etc. Keep a journal and rate how you feel when you try the different steps. Try to consistently address your fear by being aware of your feelings and taking small steps toward achieving your goals. Overcoming your fear takes time and practice.

FEAR OR LOVE

Neale Donald Walsch, author of *Conversations with God,* says, "All human actions are motivated at their deepest level by one of two emotions, fear or love." He goes on to say, "Fear is the energy that contracts, closes down, draws in, runs, hides, hoards, harms. Love is the energy which expands, opens ups, sends out, stays, reveals, shares, heals."

So, in every situation, in every decision placed before you, you have the opportunity to ask, "Am I going to choose fear or love in this situation?" Remember that love means both love for yourself and compassion for the world. What would you do in the challenging situations in your life if you chose love? For a person who has let go of the noise, each precious moment is new—a new canvas of possibilities.

We think you will agree that approaching the world with possibility instead of fear could lead you to interesting places. That doesn't mean that you would do crazy things like walk down dark alleys in rough neighborhoods, or that you would do something that is unsafe; yet living your life with possibility in mind, as opposed to fear, could stretch your view of what lies ahead for you. It could result in you breaking the surface tension of the sea, to breathe a fresh breath. How wonderful would that be? How cool would it be to live each moment fully present, fully open to the possibilities of the world? This is what overcoming fear does for us. This is what turning fear into spears gets us. It gets us our true selves.

We're not going to pretend that surfing is one hundred percent safe. There is some danger involved in surfing. Fear is a mechanism for dealing with danger. We get pumped with adrenaline so we can deal with the bear we found in our cave. Fight or flight, right? Years ago, a friend was surfing with her boyfriend and the leash wrapped around her neck and pulled her down into the water. She didn't have the benefit of a surf school, a friend, or this book to guide her. Nonetheless, she pushed through that fear and now finds solace in the surf whenever she can. Despite its dangers, surfing's potential benefits far outweigh the potential risks.

Surfing serves as a metaphor for life. Its ultimate lesson: Can you stand calm, amidst the chaos, and take a bite out of joy? Can you—despite your fears—try something you never thought you could do? Can you transform your fear into intelligent concern?

Life isn't easy at times and, trust us, surfing isn't easy either. You are going to fall, many times. You are going to want to give up. Your arms will be tired. The waves will look big and menacing. You'll say to yourself, "What the hell am I doing this for?"

But if you want it enough, the promise of joy, fun, and liberation will push you to keep trying. Surfing demands that you face your fears, no matter how big or small—face the chaos and find your

there, waiting for you. As you embark on a transformational quest, ask yourself the same questions a beginning surfer might ask:

Do I really want this? Do I want it enough that I would dive in fully, risk failure, and be in it for the long haul? Do I have the discipline to carry it through? Am I willing to invest my time, money, and energy into this? Am I willing to risk the comfortable life for the juicy life? Am I willing to keep trying, regularly, in the pursuit of my goal? Do I want it enough to just try it once—even if I don't become a surfer?

surfing serves as a metaphor for life its ultimate lesson: can you stand calm, amidst the chaos, and take a bite out of joy?

centered place amidst it all. Many of us want to feel centered. We want the serenity to be able to deal with life and its chaos with calm intelligence. And this is exactly what surfing teaches us.

Like life, surfing has the potential to bring you both incredible joy and gut-wrenching pain. The challenge, the seeming chaos, the fear of pain, the fear of inadequacy, the fear of what people might think—it's all out there at your local beach break. The stage where you can try to conquer fear is out

Whether or not you actually become a surfer is inconsequential. What's important is the process of overcoming the fear. As you read the stories of the women in this book, you'll begin to answer some of these questions for yourself. Many of them talk about how they deal with their fears. Perhaps you'll draw some inspiration and wisdom from their experiences. The ultimate choice is fear or love.

We wish you miles of glassy waves, endless smiles, and epic rides. We wish you love.

A rational look at the possibility of a shark attack

"And truthfully, this [going back to surfing] isn't false courage. To constantly dwell on what might happen would totally suck the joy out of the sport. Besides, it's like asking, What if the roller coaster comes off the track? (It has happened.) What if the horse throws you? What if you get hit in the head with the baseball, puck, or golf ball? Or you get bitten by a rattler while hiking? Life is full of what-ifs. You can't let it hold you back. If you do, you're not really living at all . . ."

—Bethany Hamilton,
fourteen-year-old pro surfer and shark bite victim

Let's face it, sharks have gotten a bad rap, haven't they? Hollywood has not made them the most loved animals in the world. The truth of the matter is, sharks think we taste bad. There are a whole lot of good things to eat out in the ocean and we aren't one of them. In fact, Shark Info, an international organization focused on providing accurate information about sharks, calls dangerous encounters between sharks and humans *shark accidents*, as opposed to *shark attacks*. Nonetheless, people have had some serious and deadly encounters with sharks over the last hundred years, so it makes sense to discuss the topic. While we're clearly not experts on this issue, we've gathered some thoughts and facts about sharks (below) to help quell your fears.

"Considering other sources of danger in day-to-day living, shark attacks are certainly overrated and do not deserve the attention given to them, as a comparison with daily accidents can demonstrate: For example, every year in the U.S. and Canada alone, around 40 people are involved in deadly accidents with pigs—this is four times (!) more than the worldwide number of shark attacks."

—Shark Info International Media Services

"Of the more then 350 shark species, about 80 percent are unable to hurt people or rarely encounter people."

—The Center for Shark Research

"In the United States, one is 30 times more likely to be killed by lightning than a shark."

—California Academy of Sciences (website)

Sharks versus Home Improvement

Total # of injuries in the United States in 1996:

Buckets: 10,907

Toilets: 43,687

Shark-related injury: 18

—Source of home injury data: U.S. Consumer Product Safety Commission, Washington, D.C., USA (1997)

—Source of shark attack data: International Shark Attack File

---

Total # of lightning strikes in the United States, 1959–90: 5,528

Total # of lightning fatalities in the United States, 1959–90: 1,505

—Source of lightning data: Hollifield, J. 1991. National Summary of Lightning, 1990. U.S. Dept. of Commerce, National Climatic Data Center, Asheville, NC, p. 11

Total # of shark attacks in the United States, 1959–90: 336

Total # of shark attack fatalities in the United States, 1959–90: 12

—Source of shark attack data: International Shark Attack File, 3 February 1998

"Overall, it has been estimated that some 100 million sharks have been taken annually from the sea in recent years. Most of these are landed from multi-species fisheries or taken as bycatch, rather than caught by fisheries targeting sharks . . . The sharks are among the most important 'keystone' marine species. This means they have a significant role in maintaining the equilibrium of the marine environment."

—The Shark Trust

Sure, we can throw a lot of facts at you, but we all know that the fear of sharks is beyond rational. It touches us at a primal level. Toilets don't have big sharp teeth and most of us don't go around looking at the sky in fear of lightning. If you got really honest with them, most surfers would admit that they have some fear of shark accidents, regardless of all the statistics. So how do we deal with it?

Making sure you don't strap bloody fish to your leash is one good way. Surfing in groups is also helpful. Another way is to have so much fun that the thought of a misguided shark doesn't even enter your consciousness. Surf with friends, laugh, and work on improving your surfing. If the thought of a shark accident does enter your mind, just remember how dangerous toilets are.

nterview:

Nani Naish

Student/Surf Diva Surf School
surf instructor, age twenty-three
San Diego, California

Nani is a student and surf instructor and
the daughter of a world-class surfer and
windsurfer. Here, among other things, we
get to hear about the effect she had on two
women from New York City. Her openness and stoke shines through.

Have you ever done anything dangerous in your life? Besides surfing? Well, my mom is a hunter and I've gone on some pretty crazy, dangerous hunting trips. We'd go hiking in the Molokai Mountains, trying to get deer and stuff, bears . . . I've done rock climbing, but I've never jumped out of a plane.

Some people consider rock climbing or surfing dangerous. Did you ever have any fear about them? Surfing? Oh yeah, all the time. But you gotta push yourself to certain limits, you know? Like, I think fear is a good thing. It makes you stronger and you find your limits. My dad, for instance, he windsurfs Jaws in extremely large waves and he's in dangerous situations regularly. [Jaws,

or P'eahi, is a break on the north shore of Hawaii known for its incredibly large size and high winds.] And I ask, "Weren't you scared?" And he's like, "Yeah, but that adrenaline rush . . ." [It's] kind of what he's lived for.

What do you do about fear? You catch a big wave or you have a big wipeout and then you kind of just paddle into shore and you kind of sit down and realize how powerful Mother Nature is. Makes you respect it a little more.

We have this theory that women who try surfing and somehow conquer that fear, and continually conquer it, somehow are able to do things they didn't think they could

do. They can push through other fears. Do you think that's true? Definitely, with anything in life. It will definitely help you. It's helped me. Just to try new things in general. For women especially, it's hard to be so independent sometimes. When doing a sport like surfing, maybe even any sport, you conquer it and you're like, "Wow, I can really do this on my own."

How long have you been teaching surfing lessons? I've been teaching for about five years, but I've only been doing Surf Diva for one. It's been really amazing with Surf Diva. Like, women empowering women is an amazing thing . . . A lot of times you have boyfriends teaching [their girlfriends]. And that just

sucks. It's like, "Hey, stand up, just do it." And the girl is like, "I can't do it!" It's just way more fun when it's just a bunch of girls together having a good time.

Do have any stories about women who took your surfing classes and then made some changes in their lives as a result, or is that a stretch? Yeah, I had these two women in my surf lesson. They flew to San Diego right after 9/11. Both of their husbands had died in the towers. And they needed something, something out of the ordinary. And they came and they were really down. It was really sad, and you didn't know what to say to them. They were a little bit larger, and I worked with them. And by the time they stood up, after the

second day, they had the biggest smiles on their faces. And they were like, "Thank you SO much for this. . . ." They were just enlightened by it. And they actually moved from New York to California and just got in the water and became full-on little surfer chicks.

This book is for women who are thinking about trying surfing. What advice do you have for them? I think women should definitely get out there and try it. And screw the guys who are telling them not to. It's just so stupid. It's different out here than in Hawaii. In Hawaii, a lot of women try to surf. There are so many girls out in the water. Maybe 'cause we're just surrounded by the ocean. You know, I went to California and

there were, like, no girls surfing. Why? Maybe they're like, "Well, I'm scared and the guys do it . . ." That's the stupidest thing I've ever heard. They should just try it. It definitely changes people's lives.

OK, a last question for you. What does surfing mean to you? What part does it play in your life? Well, the ocean is my religion. You know? Surfing is my church. It's definitely taken me to amazing places that I totally never would have gone to if I didn't surf. It's made me meet so many amazing people. Yeah, the ocean is my religion. It's where I go every day to meditate and pray. And teaching surfing is just . . . I love it. I love sharing that joy. I love seeing people's smiles.

CHAPTER

5

BASIC TRAINING

THE SEEMING CHAOS OF PERFECT ORDER

On the first day of your tennis lesson, your instructor might show you how to hold the racket, tell you the rules of the game, and talk to you about the various lines on the court. Imagine then that during your lesson—just as you feel like you're starting to understand the rules—the net suddenly moves toward you at great speed, the lines begin to move sideways, and the other play-

it will begin to feel as familiar as your favorite hangout

ers jump into your court to hit your ball and theirs. In essence, this is what learning to surf can feel like during your first year of surfing.

The ocean is a fantastic place. It surrounds us and connects us with billions of people from around the world. What is challenging about the ocean is that it's in a constant state of flux. As you wade in, you'll feel the pull of the undertow suck-

ing water out toward the sea. If the conditions are windy and choppy, all your experience with how waves break will be thrown out the window as waves crash from every imaginable direction. You'll feel rip currents flowing in different directions, and you'll feel the water rise as waves form and then crash toward the shore. The combination of all this sensory input and rapidly changing conditions can be very disorienting.

The end result is that many people feel completely out of control, hesitant, and powerless. Much of this has to do with the stress caused by not knowing what's coming next—and from which direction it's coming. It can feel like pure chaos.

What makes things more challenging is that conditions are constantly changing—from minute to minute, beach to beach, high tide to low tide, from weather condition to weather condition. How then can you begin to feel safe and confident amidst such drama?

Despite how it sometimes feels, the ocean is not purely chaotic. There is a delicious order to it all. With experience, practice, and curious attention, you'll begin to notice patterns in all the chaos. You'll notice that there is a particular area

A typical "popping up" exercise that is used by most surf schools.

Surfing instruction in the "classroom" at Las Olas Surf Safaris. Note the writing on the board: DON'T PANIC!

of the beach where a channel of water pulls out to sea and allows for easier passage into the lineup. You'll see an area where the wave seems to rise suddenly because of the reef underneath. You'll even begin to "feel" when a wave is forming on the outside so you can paddle to the precise spot and paddle into that pretty left. Learning to understand how waves break is called *developing your wave knowledge*. With years of practice, your wave knowledge will become second nature. You'll know how your home break works on certain kinds of swells; you'll know whether high tide or low tide is good for that particular spot; and you'll know where to place yourself in the lineup to catch the most waves. After a while, you'll start to feel at home in the water. It will begin to feel as familiar as your favorite hangout and the fear of the unknown and the unexpected will fade.

HOW TO DEVELOP YOUR WAVE KNOWLEDGE

Two qualities will help you navigate the fickle nature of the sea. The first is to practice calmness amidst chaos. With the cacophony of sounds and spray in the sea, you'll need to practice relaxing your muscles, your mind, and your heartbeat. This slowing down allows you more oxygen, for your muscles and for your brain. We all know that you can't learn anything when you're terrified. So breathe slowly and deeply and practice slowing yourself in relation to the chaos. The greater the chaos, the slower your breathing.

The second quality needed here is to cultivate your curiosity by noticing everything and asking about it. Surfers make a thousand evaluations of ocean conditions every time we surf. We are constantly, and often subconsciously, evaluating and reevaluating our position in the water, the

with years of practice, your wave knowledge will become second nature

strength and direction of the rip current, and the ideal positioning for the next wave. Paddle out with experienced surfers and notice things; ask why they do what they do and why they choose to do that particular thing at that particular moment. They often don't realize that all these evaluations and adjustments have become second nature.

This is what we hope for you. We hope that you'll traverse through all the chaos to find the perfect order—and that understanding the sea will become second nature to you.

UNDERSTANDING WAVE ETIQUETTE

It might seem odd to speak of etiquette, out there on the wild and untamed sea. Yet the need for rules or guidelines becomes pretty clear once you're out there among all the chaos, people, and flying boards.

Notice how the male surfer on the right is already standing and is closer to the whitewater. This wave is clearly a *right* (the open face of the wave is moving toward the right, from the surfer's perspective). The female surfer has *dropped in* on his wave and blocked him from moving toward the face. This is a cardinal sin in surfing.

The rule regarding not dropping in—or wave etiquette, as some people call it—can only be understood if you understand how waves break. As we've mentioned before, waves generally break as a right, a left, or both ways. A *left* is a wave that breaks from right to left, from the vantage point of the surfer when she is facing the beach. A *right* breaks from left to right, from the same vantage point.

Here's how the rule works. The surfer closest to the peak, or the breaking whitewater, has the right-of-way over a surfer who is farther out on the shoulder of the wave. The peak and the area directly next to it are the steepest part of the wave. The closer you are to it, the more likely you are to have the right-of-way on a particular wave.

To make things even more exciting, sometimes waves break in both directions. These waves, often called *A-frames*, break both right and left. There's a ridable shoulder on each side of the wave. You can call it right or left if you are closest to peak, the top of the *A*.

A second part of the right-of-way rule has more to do with timing than your position on the wave. This rule states that the first surfer standing on the wave has the right-of-way over others who are still paddling. This is a great rule for longboarders. A longboarder can catch a wave sooner than a shortboarder because of a longboard's ability to maintain momentum and float on top of the wave before it gets really steep. So, if you are the first one standing on the wave, it is your wave—even if another surfer is on the *inside of you*, closer to the peak.

And when you remember that most surfboards are hard and have sharp fins, you begin to understand why the biggest danger in surfing is other surfers—not drowning or getting bitten by a wayward shark. On the one hand, the absence of strict rules is what makes surfing such a carefree sport. On the other hand, without some rules surfers could easily run into each other while navigating the high seas.

There are really only a few rules when it comes to surfing. Here are the most important ones:

1. Don't *drop in* on someone and share the waves.
2. Try to hang onto your board so it doesn't hit other people.
3. Try to paddle around the break so that you're not in the way of oncoming surfers.

Now, just because you are in the right spot on the wave to be awarded the right-of-way does not mean the wave is automatically yours. You must take the extra step of claiming it as your own by saying something like, "I got left!" or "Going right!" and then paddling your heart out. This *calling off* is what experienced surfers do when they want a wave and they find others preparing to catch the same wave. However, you very rarely see inexperienced surfers calling off experienced surfers. It takes a lot of guts to do such a thing.

Your skill might not be at the level where it makes sense for you to call off another surfer. It may not make sense because calling for a left assumes that you can actually catch the wave, make the drop-in, stand up, and then ride down the face of the wave while making a quick left turn. It may take a several months to a year of surfing before you can pull that off consistently. In the meantime, you'll most likely be riding straight down the face of the wave and riding straight toward the beach. If that's where you're at in your development, don't bother calling off experienced surfers. They can make it down the face and go left or right respectively—and they might get their feathers ruffled if you call out "Left!" and then proceed to go straight down the wave. To them, what you've done is essentially to waste a good ridable shoulder.

Once you have the skills to ride the face of the wave and you've called off other surfers, one of three things will happen: they'll pull out and stop paddling, they'll keep paddling until they're sure you're actually going to catch the wave, or they'll drop in on you. If they do drop in on you, that is considered bad etiquette. People get dropped in on all the time, mostly by beginners who either don't know the rules or haven't internalized them enough to look both ways before catching a wave. If you do end up dropping in on someone, the

the absence of strict rules is what makes surfing such a carefree sport

proper response is to acknowledge your mistake and say something like, "Hey, sorry. I didn't see you." Most surfers, being of generally good nature after years of being calmed by Mother Ocean, will not make a big deal of it. Some surfers have been known to go ballistic over such an occurrence, but they are the exception and not the rule.

Each wave is like a fleeting gem. Each one is different, brilliant, and transitory. There will never be another one like the one you're paddling into. As a result, if the waves happen to be particularly nice, and there is a sizable crowd of surfers in a relatively small area, there will be some competition over who gets to ride these five-second gems. Some surfers will get upset if you go after one of these waves, then ruin it by falling off your board. Most surfers are not greedy about waves. They understand that although each wave is a gem, there are millions of

beaches, each littered with thousands of gems crashing on their shores every day.

Our advice is to approach the ocean as an unlimited source of abundance. The world will not end if you *eat it* (wipe out) on a wave that someone else wanted. Remember that each one of those surfers was once a beginner and they ate it many, many times in order to become proficient.

The fastest learners are the ones who go for wave after wave—with due respect for other surfers—falling sometimes, but making it other times. Remember, you have the right to make mistakes. You have the right to be a beginner. It does not make you a lesser person, nor does it say anything about your goodness or proficiency. It simply means that you're new to the sport. Contrary to popular belief, there is no shortage of waves in the world.

HOW TO PADDLE

Imagine that you are a dolphin. You are slippery and gray. You have a broad smile and a jovial disposition. The ocean is your oyster. You achieve great speed with minimum effort. Your body is perfectly symmetrical and hydrodynamic. This is the state you're trying to achieve when you're paddling.

Paddling is its own art form. In fact, there is an entire sport dedicated to surf paddling. Proper paddling technique can make a huge difference in your time in the water. There are essentially two times when you paddle in surfing: when you're trying to make it out past the breakers, and when

you're trying to catch a wave. Let's start by learning how to paddle out past the breakers.

Centering yourself

If you've ever seen a wind-tunnel test that measures the aerodynamics of a car, you know how important it is to streamline an object moving

the fastest learners are the ones who go for wave after wave

through a medium like air or water. This is why an arrow moves more easily through the air than a piece of pie, for example. The arrow is more "slippery," meaning it does not have a lot of surfaces that make contact with the air to slow it down.

When paddling, we aim to minimize the number of surfaces that stick out (like arms and legs that are dragging in the water) and achieve the right position between the nose and the tail of the board. The idea is to *center* yourself on the board, from left to right and from nose to tail. Since your body is heavier in the area around your hips, it is very important that your hips are in the right place from side to side and from nose to tail. Leaning your hip just an inch or two too far to your left will cause the board to tilt slightly, making the board much slower over the surface of the water. Placing your hips and body too far forward will cause the nose of the board to *pearl*—to go slightly underwater,

Here Mary shows us what happens if you try to
paddle with your body too far back on the board.

Same problem, except this time Mary is too far forward.

which slows you down considerably. In the same regard, placing your body a little too far back will cause the tail of the board to sink. If your tail is slightly underwater on a longboard, you won't be able to catch a wave very effectively.

Your body should be like an arrow, centered on the *stringer* (the wooden strip that runs down the middle of a board). Your back should be slightly arched, head forward, and your toes should be on the board. A lot of beginners tend to spread their legs a bit when paddling and drag their feet off the side of the board. This is like driving a moving truck instead of a Ferrari. Either point your toes and rest them on the back of the board or prop your feet up by your toes.

Lining up

Now that we've got you centered, it's time to position yourself correctly on the wave. Your arms are the paddles and your board is the boat. On a longboard, your first priority is to line yourself up in precisely the direction you want to go. Sometimes a surfer will point the board diagonally while they're trying to go straight. This is essentially a waste of effort. If you're paddling out to the waves, you want your board positioned perpendicular to the whitewater lines that are advancing. In the same respect, if you turn your board around to catch a wave, point your board directly at the beach—perpendicular to the oncoming wave—and then center yourself and paddle. If you've graduated to catching waves before they have broken, then it makes sense to line your board up at a slight angle to the line of the wave. For example, if you're catching a left, you should point your board at a slight diagonal, with the nose of the board pointing toward the left.

This diagonal positioning is only to be used when you're catching a wave that has not broken. When catching whitewater, point your board directly at the beach.

Digging In

OK, now you're centered on your board—side to side and nose to tail. You've got yourself lined up in the direction you want to go. The last thing to do is to dig in and paddle.

The idea behind the second type of paddling (paddling to catch a wave) is to get the surfboard moving at roughly the same speed as the oncoming wave. To catch a wave two things must happen: you must get enough speed to be close to the speed of the oncoming wave, and you must be positioned in a part of the wave that is steep enough to carry you.

There is some law of physics that says an object at rest will stay at rest until acted upon by a force. Conversely, a moving object will keep moving in the same direction until acted upon by some outside force. So, if you happen to be in space and you throw a baseball, that baseball will keep going in the direction you threw it forever, or until it hits something or is pulled in a particular direction by some planet's gravity. So what in the heck does this have to do with surfing?

Notice how this surfer has her body lined up, her back arched, and her arms fully extended forward. She digs in . . .

. . . and pushes lots of water backward. This technique will get her moving quickly.

Mary O, showing us how to catch whitewater.

Once you get your surfboard moving fast enough, it wants to keep moving until it is slowed down by something. That something could be your feet dragging off the side, the friction caused by the seaweed that's caught on your leash, etc. So your main job is to get the board moving so that it begins to have its own momentum.

To get it moving, you've got to power it with deep strokes similar to the crawl or freestyle stroke in swimming. Because something at rest wants to stay at rest, getting it from a standstill to moving is the hardest part.

Place your fingers and thumbs together and cup each hand slightly to form a paddle with your hands. Start with slow strokes that dig deep into the water and push lots of water toward the tail of your board. Alternate your arms—right, left, right, left . . .

Once you've got the board moving a bit, start taking quicker strokes to keep up with the now-blazing speed of your board. Now you've got momentum. You can use this momentum to paddle out past the breakers or to paddle into your next wave. Keep practicing in order to build up your muscles and to refine your form and positioning. The more you paddle the more you'll notice how slight variations in your body position on the board and in your stroke make a huge difference in how fast you can paddle.

CATCHING WHITEWATER

There are waves, and then there are waves that have broken. A wave that has broken has reached its maximum steepness—leading to the lip of the wave curling over, falling in itself, and then doing so down the face of the wave.

The unbroken part of the wave is the part that most experienced surfers are seeking. Their desire is not to ride the wave straight toward the beach, but instead to ride it sideways from left to right (or vice versa). Riding sideways across the face of a wave is an indescribable feeling. In order to get you to that feeling, most surf schools agree that it makes sense to start you out riding whitewater. Here's why it's easier to start out by catching whitewater:

1. You don't have to paddle past all the breakers to get out to where the waves start breaking (the lineup). Depending on the conditions, this can be very difficult and physically taxing.

2. You are less likely to pearl when catching whitewater. There is no steepness to a broken wave and therefore very little chance that the nose of your board would be thrust underwater.

3. It's easier to catch whitewater. Your paddling speed and positioning is not really that important when catching whitewater. The main difference is that when you catch an unbroken wave, the force that propels you forward is your paddling coupled with gravity as you ride down the face. When you catch whitewater, the force that's propelling you forward is the actual water itself.

4. Catching whitewater allows you to feel the joy of being moved by a wave much sooner than trying to catching unbroken waves. Catch a lot of whitewater waves before you try to stand up.

5. The experienced surfers are done with the wave by the time the wave becomes whitewater. This helps you avoid getting in the way of other surfers.

6. Catching whitewater gives you more time to stand up.

But there is a downside to catching whitewater. Whitewater is basically water moving in a hundred different directions as it is pushed toward the beach. So, by nature it's a bit more unpredictable. When you first catch the wave, you'll feel this vortex of energy, like a thousand tiny white horses, pushing you this way and that from many directions. You won't be able to see because of all the water rushing around you, and you'll be in for a bumpy first few seconds of your ride. This can feel very disorienting—but you can take solace in knowing that the bumpiness of the ride only lasts a few seconds before it starts to smooth out.

How to do it

Walk yourself and your board out into the water. As each whitewater wave comes, gently pick up your board by its middle and jump the board over the wave. Plant your feet in the sand, walk out farther, and repeat until you've reached chest level in the water.

Now, when the next wave arrives, jump the board over and then immediately turn yourself and the board toward the beach. To do this quickly, hold the back of the

Mary is too far forward on the board, and the nose of the board is starting to "pearl" or sink into the water. Correct this by inching backwards or arching your back.

board down as you bring the tip of the board around. Point your board precisely perpendicular to the beach and climb onto the board.

Now with all the excitement, most beginners fall into the same trap at this stage. They climb or hurl themselves onto the board and start paddling immediately. Nine times out of ten this leads to a very well-meaning and determined surfwoman laying way too far back, too far forward, or leaning to one side of the board. Too far back and you can see the nose of the board sticking out of the water. Too far forward and you can feel free to bet all your burrito money on the high probability that when the wave arrives, this surfer is going to do some major pearling. The wave will thrust the board down underwater, the surfer will slide down the board into the water, and then the board will literally be shot out of the back of the wave. While this business of pearling is very disconcerting to the new and nubile surfer, it is a source of great amusement for the local vultures sitting on the beach.

This is all to encourage you to take one extra step before paddling intensely for the wave. As soon as you climb onto the board, take an extra second or two to line your body up properly. Remember our lesson on hydrodynamics: The more lined up you are—like an arrow, strung and ready for its target—the more likely you are to catch and eventually stand up on your wave.

This is when our discussion about momentum pops right into your brain and you remember to start with slow, deep, and powerful paddles. Your job is to get your nine-foot board moving at a similar speed to that of the wave.

As those thousand tiny white horses approach, you glance over your shoulder to see how close the whitewater is, and then you begin to speed up your paddling. The wave comes, and you're tossed around a bit. At this point it makes sense to stop paddling and to hold on tight, with two hands, to the rails of your board, until you clear out of the rambling mess of whitewater. In a second or so, you'll be pushed out in front of the wave where it's a bit calmer. Now you'll get this huge smile on your face as the rush of being propelled begins to sink in. This is the same rush that we had as children when we caught our first wave on that little orange boogie board. Savor the smile; you've caught whitewater!

REGARDING TURTLES AND DUCKS

At some point, early in your surfing life, you're going to want to get to the promised land—or more accurately, the promised water. This is the area of the surf break where the waves are forming before they break, known as the *outside* or the *lineup*. It can be a very meditative place, beyond the breakers. Not being able to make it out to the lineup can damage your ego. Reaching the outside is your reward for all that paddling. It is also your entry into the exclusive club of experienced surfers who have also made it out past the breakers. Somehow, sitting out there with "real surfers" gives you a feeling of accomplishment, pride, and membership.

If you're riding a longboard, and you want to make it out there, you're going to have to turn into a turtle.

Turtles

Longboards are wonderful, so stable and graceful. They make catching and standing on waves so much easier than a shortboard does. The major drawback of a longboard is that it is so big that

> sitting out there with "real surfers" gives you a feeling of accomplishment

you cannot push it through or under a wave like a shortboard. When the water is shallow enough to stand in, you can simply bend your knees and jump your board over an approaching wave. If the water is a bit deeper, or the wave is too big to jump over, the best thing to do is to turn turtle.

The idea behind turning turtle is to reduce the amount of surface area that is being hit by the wave. The less surface area hit, the less you are going to be pushed backward by the wave. Remember, you are trying to advance forward and out to the lineup as quickly as possible. Each time you let a wave pummel you, you are going to be sent backward, thereby making your paddle out more arduous. Turning turtle effectively turns you into a very slippery and hydrodynamic racecar, allowing the wave to pass over you without too much fanfare. Here are the steps for turning turtle.

1. Look at the broken wave ahead and paddle like a raging bull straight toward it. Although this doesn't seem to make much sense, the idea here is to advance as much as possible and to get some forward momentum before the wave pushes you backward.

2. Immediately before the wave arrives, grab the rails of your board, flip the board over, and hold on to the board as tight as possible.

you've battled all your fear or insecurity demons and tamed the sea

3. Keep your body and board close together and horizontal as the wave passes over you. Turn the board and yourself over as soon as the wave passes. Begin paddling immediately with slow deep strokes, repeat, and rinse.

Ducks

If you have a board that is shorter than eight feet and has a pointy nose, you do have the option of becoming a duck. Ducks can slide underwater in one graceful move without ruffling their feathers. In your quest to make it to the outside, this could come in very handy.

A smaller board can avoid the powerful part of a wave simply by ducking underneath it and popping out on the other side as it passes. In order to duck-dive, try these steps:

1. Paddle hard, straight toward the oncoming wave.

2. Right before it smacks you in the face, grab the rails and shove the nose of the board down hard at a 45° angle as you push one knee into the board. Your entire body weight should be pushing down at three points: one hand on each of the rails and one knee in the center of the board.

3. As the wave passes, stop pushing with your hands and let your knee do most of the pushing. The nose of your board will suddenly be pushed upward. Hold onto the rails tightly as you and the board are rushed to the surface and popped out of the back of the wave.

With some practice, duck-diving can be really fun and can actually propel you forward.

HOW TO STAND UP

Remember your first time riding a two-wheeler bicycle amid cheers and clapping? Remember your first car, or your very first kiss? Catching and standing up on a wave for the very first time could go down on your list of cherished memories. It is pure bliss, because you've battled all your fear or insecurity demons and tamed the sea, if for one brief moment, and you are standing smiling at the helm. If you consider it for a moment, it seems a bit impossible. You are actually standing on moving

An underwater view of a great duck dive.

You too could feel this good.

water and being pushed forward at the speed of your grin. The feeling is so deep that, for many beginners, arms are thrown automatically up in a victory pose, like Mary Lou Retton winning Olympic gold. If you'd like to get to that feeling sooner rather than later, read on.

Determining your stance

At some point, early on in your surfing career, you'll be asked a question that might seem like a jest. Someone might say, "Cool, you're a surfer, huh? Are you goofy or regular?" Rest assured, this question has nothing to do with how silly you are or how consistent your bowel movements are. Your interlocutor is basically asking you which foot you place in the front when you ride. As we mentioned earlier, if you ride more naturally with your left foot forward, you're a *regular-footer*. If you ride with your right foot forward, you're a *goofy-footer*. Either way is totally acceptable. It's mostly just a matter of what feels more comfortable to you.

To determine your stance, try these two steps:

1. Without thinking, put one foot on a skateboard and push off the pavement with the other. If you put your right foot on the skateboard and that feels more natural, then you're a goofy-footer (and vice versa).
2. Lie on the ground and practice popping up to your feet without using your knees. Which foot naturally goes forward?

Once you've got your stance, you can start practicing the infamous pop-up.

The mechanics of a pop-up

Grace is a hard thing to achieve. Nonetheless, we just keep striving for it. To have grace while standing up on a slippery surfboard moving through slippery water is a bit much to ask on your first day out. Our aim here is to teach your body, to build the cellular memory, to stand in the proper way from the start. Although it takes a bit longer to stand from the start, it helps prevent bad habits from forming.

The proper way to stand up on a surfboard is in one smooth and graceful motion, lovingly known as the *pop-up*. To do it properly is to set yourself up in a relaxed and commanding position as early as possible. The more you focus on the pop-up throughout your surfing career, the more it will improve your overall surfing.

"Rise up nimbly, and go on your strange journey to the ocean of meanings . . ."—Rumi

Now let's focus on what you *should* do. To execute a pretty pop-up requires doing it, over and over and over. Do it on the beach, do it at home on your living room carpet, and do it in your bedroom. Whatever you do, just do it a whole bunch. Wake up in the morning and do thirty pop-ups before you have breakfast. Do twenty before you wade into the surf. Pop-ups are a lot more fun

Mary O and her perfect pop-up.

than push-ups—and there's a deeper purpose behind the whole exercise.

To explain the pop-up more efficiently, we've outlined the steps for a goofy-footer, below. If you're a regular-footer, just replace the word "right" wherever you see the word "left".

Lie on your stomach on the floor, or on your surfboard in the sand. Place your right palm beneath your right shoulder (facing fingers forward) and keep your elbow tucked into your body. Place the heel of your left hand at your left hip and point your fingers to the left. Prop your feet as you curl your toes onto the board (or floor). Inhale, and then on your exhale push on the board (or floor) with a quick and powerful shove (like the kind of shove you'd give a schoolyard bully). As you are pushing, simultaneously twist your hips counterclockwise (clockwise for regular-footers) as you shove your right foot forward and underneath your body. At this point, you should lean your weight backward so you don't fall forward as the wave is pushing you. Make sure your feet are about shoulder-width apart and that they are both pointing sideways (toes pointing to the left side of the board). If you've done it properly, your knees will have never touched the board and your feet will automatically be in the right position to ride. No adjustments should be necessary. The whole thing should be one movement, which takes less than a second to accomplish.

What you want to avoid is the flailing of arms, the use of the knees as an intermediate step, and the face-forward body positioning that so often characterizes the mistakes that beginners make. Here are some illustrations of what *not* to do.

Common surf poses to avoid when standing up

The Sneeze at the Knees

Notice how our determined heroine is using her knees to stand up. Using your knees actually sets you off balance and wastes precious time.

The Soldier Pose

If you stand up and find your two feet pointing forward, something has gone amiss. When your feet are pointed forward, your board becomes like a wobbly tightrope. You lose your ability to balance and your ability to turn the board.

THE SNEEZE AT THE KNEES

NO KNEES!

THE SOLDIER POSE

FEET SHOULD NOT FACE FORWARD UNLESS YOU ARE "HANGIN' TEN"

FEET TOO FAR APART!

STOOD UP BEFORE SHE CAUGHT THE WAVE

The Splitz

While it may seem like spreading your legs out gets you more stability, you should test this theory of yours. Spread your legs out and have someone try and push you over. Now bend your knees slightly and place your feet about shoulder-width apart. You're much more stable this way. Doing the splits may be good for yoga, but not for surfing.

The Ambitious Amy

Yes, Amy has a big smile on her face. Yet notice that the wave has passed without taking her along with it. Make sure that the wave is moving you forward before you stand up.

HOW TO BAIL

Surfing small to medium waves is not especially dangerous. In fact, you're at more risk walking down the stairs or driving in a car. Nevertheless, there are some things you can do to help prevent yourself from getting hurt.

When surfers get hurt, it usually has something to do with getting hit by their own board or someone else's board. With all that water moving around and those fiberglass boards with fairly sharp fins, carelessness could lead to some cuts and bruises. So, in addition to learning how to ride, we'll help you figure out how to fall.

Bailing is the art of falling or jumping off your board without hurting yourself or others in your wake. The first thing to remember is to always be aware of your surroundings. We cannot stress this point enough. Remember that waves move toward the beach, so you never want to place yourself in front of a board that is loose and traveling toward the beach. Many a surfista has been hurt or yelled at because she jumped off her board and let the board run into another surfer. When paddling out,

Since there are no other people around who might get hit by the board, Mary puts as much distance as she can between her and her board by kicking it forward as she goes backward.

riding, or catching waves, always look in all four directions to make sure no one is in the way. You could get so focused on catching and riding waves that you forget about who or what may be around you. Sometimes, when surfers are paddling out and a wave breaks in front of them, they let their board go without looking behind them. This is a big no-no. If you let your board go, it could easily bounce off the head of the person paddling behind you. Worse yet, since surfboards are fragile, you could ding someone's board. Most surfers would rather get a cut on their bodies than get a ding on their board. Remember that each time you let your board go it becomes a projectile moving at great speed. If you keep your board under control, close to you most of the time, it is less likely to hit you or someone else. If you must let your board go, make sure there's no one around first.

Bailing out when you're riding a wave is a bit trickier. In the moment, there will be much excitement. Your job will be to maintain some level-headedness as you are riding the wave. As you are riding, look ahead of you to make sure no one is ahead or nearby. If someone's there, give him or her a holler (or listen for their holler) so they can move out of your way or duck underwater. Then bend down low and try to keep riding until you pass them. If you must fall in front of someone, make sure they know you're coming and try to cover your head as you fall.

If no one is around and you're ready to bail out, just lean back and kick the board out in front of you. The aim here is to get as much distance as possible from your board. Once you're underwater, if you can touch the bottom, do so. If you can't, just cover your head and then calmly come to the surface with one hand raised (to keep from bonking your head on your floating surfboard). As you come to the top, look first for the next wave and then immediately for your board. If you have time to get your board and control it before the next wave arrives, do so. If you don't, make sure there's no one else within a twenty-foot radius, take a deep breath, and then dive under the next wave. Remember that when you're underwater, your board is a projectile flying

All smiles from this Mexican champion surfer.

around above water—so try to get control of the board as soon as possible.

DOING IT OFTEN: BUILDING ON SUCCESS

One day, when we were discussing the growth of women's surfing, a friend made the following observation: "You know, women's surfing is really becoming popular. But sometimes you come across a girl who goes out and buys a rash guard and then says, 'OK, now I'm a surfer!' You've gotta actually surf to call yourself a surfer."

While there is no definitive line between actual surfers and the people who have just tried surfing, there is a clear difference between their approaches. For some, just trying it is enough. For others, surfing becomes an insatiable thirst. We are not making any judgments here in comparing the *occasional surfer* with the *surfer*; each person tries surfing for his or her own reasons. Our only aim here is to illustrate the type of mindset that would lead someone to continuously improve as a surfer.

A woman in Brazil called surfing her "sweet vice." She had to have it. Yes, at times she'd have to leave the laundry undone, or get up extra early and risk being tired for work. Nonetheless, it was worth it. The feeling of stroking the line of the wave with one hand as she glided past was too delicious to refuse. She felt reborn with each duck dive, bettered by each wipeout. She had to have it.

Rell Sunn used to sleep with her surfboard as a youngster. She'd lay there at night, caressing the lines of the board and dreaming about her next opportunity to ride.

But let's face it—as a beginner, you may not have the same affection for the sport, and your first few months of surfing could be very frustrating. (We've spoken with surfers who've been at it for twenty years or more—and many of them still say they're learning!) So here you are, caught in the salt and spray; your arms are like sore noodles and your chest is heaving; you've just pearled your board, flipped over, and swallowed seawater; and some guy is giving you a dirty look—all this for a few seconds of standing tenuously on that big spongy board.

But at some point, your surfing scale will tip from work and embarrassment to joy and growth. When it does tip, you'll develop an energy inside. As Augusto Boal (a theater practitioner) has said, "Desire is the battery of the human ego . . ." That desire is what powers you to get out of bed at 5:30 in the morning to plunge into icy-cold water. It's that power that will lead you to paddle hard and drop in on that wave, even though you're scared. But what to do if your scale has not yet tipped?

Give yourself a chance to experience the joyous part of surfing. In order to get there, you're going to have to give yourself many opportunities. Try surfing at least three times a week for three months. Get a girlfriend-surfriend to tap on your window every morning to get you out of bed. When you're out there, go for as many waves as possible. Take another surfing class. At home, do thirty pop-ups every morning. At night, watch *The Endless Summer* by Bruce Brown. Go surfing at different breaks and try different boards. In the water, practice improving one thing at a time, like paddling or turning turtle. If you have that desire, if you want surfing to be part of your life, just keep doing it often. It may soon become more fun than work. It may soon become your sweet vice.

Seven differences between a surfer and an occasional surfer

occasional surfer	surfer
1. She surfs during her vacations.	1. She surfs every opportunity she gets. Proximity to the ocean becomes a factor in deciding where she lives.
2. It's 6:00 A.M. and she's sound asleep.	2. She's already waxed her board and is on her way to the beach.
3. She sits on her board and waits for waves.	3. She is scanning the horizon for the next wave and paddling to get into position.
4. She paddles for waves but catches few.	4. She covets every wave. She paddles deep and then fast. She wants the wave badly.
5. She doesn't make many mistakes.	5. She makes many mistakes and learns from them.
6. She sits quietly in the lineup.	6. She is curious. She asks questions and is continuously trying to improve.
7. Surfing is her hobby.	7. Surfing is her passion.

Cheryl's first surf lesson

One year after our interview, Cheryl Larsen decided to take her first lesson. She describes it here.

We introduce ourselves. All twenty-year-olds with boyfriends who surf—and me. Hmmmm . . . forty-two years old, thirty years out of the water, and terrified of the ocean. Don't want to freak anyone out, but . . .

Interestingly, I am clear and calm about my potential panic. I speak directly without drama or sugarcoating. I want this, it is time, it will be very difficult. It won't be the mechanics of getting up; it will be the anxiety that interferes. The instructor is spot-on; she sees and hears me and is appreciative of my sharing. It's a small class. I will be in her group of three (I raise my eyes to the skies in thanks).

So I put on the suit and pick up the board and start walking into the ocean. It is all too big—that I signed up, that I showed up, and that I'm now walking into the OCEAN! It is time. A not-too-tiny voice is repeating expletives as I keep moving my feet and enter the water. Ankles, knees, hips, waist—OK, that is far enough. Fortunately it is for the instructor also. We are where we need to be for the lesson.

From the time I hit the water, I'm in a serious state of emotional shock and remain there until the next day's lesson.

We are learning in whitewater, the tail end of the waves. Great. Enough to give you a lift and a ride, but theoretically less likely to drown you. And . . . shallow enough to let me feel that sharks will not be anywhere (whatever works). But on the other hand, we are learning in whitewater—constant turbulence.

I arrive fighting to stay on my feet and to refrain from panic, to move forward, stay stable, not give up my position. (What position?) I spend the first hour hyperventilating (but calmly, honest). Exhausted almost immediately—between the physical effort required to retain some sort of balance and the extreme fight-or-flight response that my submergence has triggered.

Here it comes! #%&@! Get on the board. I can't turn the #%&@-ing board. *Queen Mary* making a turn (later I learn to put some weight on the back of the board to release it from the tow of the water). Here it is! #%&@. The instructor pushes down on the back of the board and gives me a push. I scramble to push up and get my legs under me (moving in slow motion—and why haven't you been to the pool or gym in months?), tip, fall, inhale water, VERY SALTY. Whoa. Back on my feet . . . OK . . . I'm fine. Move the feet, move the feet, get back out. Whitewater, pushing back, NOT GOING BACK OR DOWN. Battle for control—of everything. Repeat for the next hour.

OK. Time to ground a bit. I talk with the instructor, tell her that I'm flailing, panicking at the incoming waves and overwhelmed by the big picture. She sees it also. I spend some time, just standing out and feeling the water, watching out for my head and critical internal organs. There are many beginners with loooonnnnng strong boards and ten-foot leashes WITHOUT a modicum of safety awareness: potential twenty-foot diameter of impending disfigurement or death. . . . Sharks are the least of your problems out here. It helps. I calm down some.

The rest of the day follows as such. I do get up on the board, acknowledge it intellectually—"Right on"—but I can't feel it. All is happening in numbness. I move on, set my own agenda, take care of myself. I'm quite tired. I get out of the water early for a break and get out whenever I need to calm down or rest.

I leave early from the class, very pleased and proud that I am caring for myself, but also alarmed at my physical exhaustion. I stop at the grocery store—buy a HUGE container of Epsom salts, bee-line home where half of the salts and I get into the tub. No one is home, thankfully, because I can't think or talk. I lie down but am too tired (freaked?) to sleep—ugh, I ache. But, "Right on." I stretch later and take another bath in the evening. Anxiety begins to grow about tomorrow's lesson. Looks like it is going to be another one of those days.

Just keep moving forward. Up the next day and down to the beach, ignoring the sick feeling in my stomach. I'm suited and ready for class. Here we go AGAIN.

Into the water. It feels a bit easier. I'm anxious but less panicked. I start working with the board as we learned the previous day and try to loosen up a bit, trust myself instead of evaluating it all. I drink a lot of ocean. We are in the shallows but some falls feel seriously underwater for me. More tired today, taking many little breaks, in and out of the water on a schedule totally divorced from the rest of the class. It's just fine—as it should be.

Mid-lesson and I start to walk out again for my salt-water dose (it's been five minutes since I swallowed a gallon . . . must get back to it). I'm moving pelvic-level through the water toward a large wave that is curling and all sound stops.

It sounds like snow falling, quiet and buffered. I'm standing calm and solid and I'm where it makes sense. The wave is large and beautiful and will not hurt me. My body can move with the water as it will. Everything is fine. It is tender and open. I'm safe.

Thirty seconds later, it's a madhouse once again. Whoa. I continue to work the board and when I get up the next time, I feel it. I push down, stand up, and RIDE the board. Right on!

I leave class an hour early. Time to go. I need to be able to walk the next day and it is still quite an effort for me to keep going in. As I drive home, with a warmth in my mind and my whole body smiling, I look to the left. I'm driving up a grade and the Pacific Ocean is there for me—stunning.

I realize that I could rule the world if I really wanted to.

Is surfing for me?

If you can swim, you can surf! Your age, size, or shape is not a barrier. Surfing is for you as long as you remember to have fun, make friends, and always try to protect our oceans.

What does *hang ten* mean?

Hanging ten is a really fun trick that you can do while riding a longboard. It's a balancing act that involves walking to the front of the board and letting all of your toes hang off of the nose while the momentum of the water on the back of your board holds you in position. Hanging twelve is something that only girls can do! ;-) Get it, girls?

Will other surfers get mad at me if I get in the way?

Do you get mad when someone cuts you off on the road? Yes? Well, surfing follows many of the same rules of the road as driving. Know before you go and you won't get in trouble with other surfers. Watch out and pay attention to those around you.

Try these simple steps:

- **Be vigilant:** Always look both ways before you drop into a wave. If in doubt, pull out.
- **Watch out:** Pay attention to those around you.
- **Share:** Let some waves go to others, even if you are in position.
- **Avoid high traffic areas:** When paddling out, stay off to the side of the takeoff zone.
- **Be friendly:** If you make a mistake and cut someone off, apologize and offer them the next wave.

How do I know what beaches are best for beginners?

Ask your instructor where the best beaches are to learn to surf. Also ask the local lifeguards or surf shop clerks where you can surf. Avoid rocky places, large crowds, piers, jetties, and places that are not patrolled by lifeguards.

What equipment do I need to be a surfer?

To get started, you need a good board that floats you and a solid leash to keep you attached to it. When learning, remember that size does matter: bigger is better. The more flotation the board has, the more waves you'll catch and the more stable the ride.

Also, a girl's gotta look good to feel good, so get a cute stay-on bathing suit, a rash guard to keep from scraping up your stomach on the board, and boardshorts to keep that cute suit in position. In water temps below seventy degrees, a wetsuit is going to keep you much warmer and happier. Get a good one that's made specifically for a girl if you want it to fit correctly and offer optimum warmth and performance. Always use waterproof sunscreen, at least SPF 15, and apply it twenty minutes before you get to the beach to give it time to soak in.

What do I do if I wear contacts?

If you wear contacts, keep your eyes tightly shut underwater. At our surf school, we recommend that students wear an old pair of contact lenses, just in case they do lose one—and to keep a spare set in the car.

I'm afraid I might be too large/too small to be a surfer. What if the wetsuit doesn't fit?

An ill-fitting wetsuit can ruin a perfect surf session (if you can't move because there is no circulation in your arms, or if water is gushing in). Wetsuits come in all shapes and sizes—from youth XS to adult 3X—and there is a perfect suit out there for you! Check out www.surfdiva.com for a full selection of women's wetsuits from size 0 to size 18. Keep your toes toasty warm with booties for your feet.

Make sure you get *women's* booties. Loose-fitting booties will fill with water and act like weights on your feet.

Is there a difference between a man's wetsuit and woman's wetsuit?

We used to have to wear men's wetsuits that had weird seams in the crotch and were way too narrow in the chest and thighs. When women's suits were first introduced, they weren't much better. They had huge hips and tiny shoulders. Nothing seemed to fit in the right places. Women's wetsuits are now shaped specifically for an athletic female figure. With newer materials and technological advances, wetsuits actually look and feel good. Hallelujah!

How long will it take me to become a good surfer?

I love this question, because everyone wants to know how long it takes to get "good." Well, that depends on what you consider "good." Our motto at Surf Diva is that the best surfer in the water is the one having the most fun.

What do I do after I take a lesson? How can I improve?

After your first lesson, keep practicing your pop-ups on dry land and work on upper-body strength and all-around flexibility. Get to the ocean as much as you can—but if you live far away, keep your stoke going by surrounding yourself with surfing books, magazines, videos, posters, and calendars. Hang out with friends who surf, and plan trips to surf camps to bring your skills to the next level. Surf the net to find out about wave conditions at your local beach, or for information on your next dream trip. Check out www.surfline.com for surf forecast and wave cams from around the world.

Izzy Tihany, the world-famous founder of Surf Diva (the first women's surf school), answers commonly asked questions about surfing.

What's the hardest part of surfing?

Don't forget to keep your expectations in line with what Mother Nature has to offer. Don't get frustrated if you aren't having a great day; maybe it's the conditions or the alignment of the stars. Don't give up. Surfing is not something you can master in a day or even a month, but you sure can have some fun along the way!

interview:

Lauri Black

Genetic counselor, age thirty-six
Pacifica, California

On a chilly morning in Pacifica, Lauri shared with us what it's like to be a pregnant surfer. Her story reveals how one woman has incorporated surfing into her emerging family.

How did you get involved in surfing?
The way I got interested in surfing was that my boss from my first job used to leave on Fridays and just be cranked up and frustrated and full of anxious energy. And he would come back on Monday morning with a big smile on his face and be all relaxed, telling me about what a great weekend he'd had in the water. He'd tell me how much fun he had surfing, and how much better he feels about life. And I'm thinking, I've got to get myself some of this. And that was only five years ago. . . . Yeah, I was thirty-one. The first day I went out . . . I was kinda surprised that I was able to stay out so long, but I was out there for four hours paddling out . . . on a fall day.

That was my first experience. I was really excited and terrified at the same time because I had no idea what I was doing or getting myself into. But fortunately some really nice guys were out there with me. It was quite an experience and I was hooked. Absolutely hooked.

Was there a lot of fear involved?
Yeah, when I was first learning, I was probably going out in conditions that I wouldn't take a beginner out in. One day I had a really bad accident. I took off on a wave, I think more out of frustration than anything else, 'cause I was trying so hard to get something and to learn and stand. So I took off on a wave and totally ate the pop-up [laughs]. And my board went flying and it got to the end of my leash and rico-

cheted and came right back at the exact moment that my head came out of the water and hit me right square on the forehead. And it was a huge fiberglass board, about ten feet long and really heavy. It didn't knock me out but it shocked me. From that point on I was very cautious and fearful. So I spent a lot of time, trying to find a balance between good fear and unhealthy fear. So it was really a good lesson. I've found that I've learned a lot of really good lessons in the water.

What did you learn about yourself, through surfing? It's a very private thing, riding a wave. I have a deeper knowledge of myself . . . in uncomfortable situations, happy situations . . . Some of the happiest moments that I

can recall have just been sitting out there, watching the otters pop up and chew on kelp, watching the dolphins go by, watching sea turtles pop their heads out at Waikiki. It's amazing stuff.

Talk about this new chapter in your life. Well, I'm pregnant; yep, I'm five months pregnant—and I'm due in January [laughter]. And it's been interesting; I've been getting so many different reactions from people, like my husband and my nurse-midwife . . . about whether or not I should continue to surf. I've always felt like, absolutely, I'm going to continue to surf until I feel personally like it's not comfortable or safe.

I remember my first prenatal visit . . . [the nurse-midwife] gets to the end of the visit and she says, "Well, do you have any questions for me?" And I said, "No." I wasn't even thinking of anything. And my husband clears his throat and says, "Should she stop surfing?" [laughter] and the nurse-midwife looks over at me and raises her eyebrows and says, "You surf?" And I say, "Yeah . . . I surf." And she says, "Well, surfing is one of those sports that we really don't recommend you do . . ." You know, her impression of surfing, and a lot of other people who

don't surf, is that it's some hard-core, kick-ass, aggressive sport—boards flying, waves crashing—and I'm out there just gliding along. It's very relaxing, sedate . . . I'm out here surfing little ankle- to knee-high waves.

So how does it work? How do you paddle with a big belly? [Laughter] It's kind of interesting. Every week I come out and it's just a little bit different. I feel like my balance is just so subtly different. Even though my board is the same and I'm the same except for my belly. It's gradually changed from not feeling any different, to feeling like I'm surfing with a grapefruit under my belly button . . . to feeling like I'm surfing with a soccer ball and then probably, shortly, a basketball . . . [laughter]. It feels different physically. You know, I don't have the stamina that I used to. But I didn't need to buy a new wetsuit—you know, they're stretchy. It doesn't feel confining or tight. My belly still hasn't gotten really that big.

I find that my husband is surfing differently. I mean, if he doesn't see me in his line of sight for more than a couple of minutes it makes him really anxious. He's very protective right now . . . which is . . . sweet. He'll be really happy when I say

I'm not surfing anymore, but he also fears how grouchy I will be [laughter]. It's a trade-off . . .

You know, it feels like I'm doing something not only good for me, but for the baby . . .

In what way? You know the peace of mind that I get when I'm out there . . . How can that not be good for the baby? I feel like I'm getting a little bit of what he's getting. I get out there, and I'm playing in the water and he's in here playing around in the water . . . so it's only fair, isn't it?

Every once in a while someone says, "Wow, you're still surfing and you're pregnant?" And my quirky response is to say, "Yeah, you gotta start 'em young!" [laughter] But I do feel that this is the first experience he's gonna have in the water, with surfing, and I don't know what he feels or his experience is, but . . . it's gotta be interesting.

The ocean is so much a part of my life and my husband's life. And it's so much a part of how we play together and stay connected that I feel like I can't imagine it not being just a natural part of the baby's life as well. So the earlier you start, the better. It's like, this is what we do, this is how we play, and this is how we're happy.

CHAPTER 6

IMPROVING AS A SURFER

Welcome to the lineup, girlfriend. It was a long way out here, we know. You made it past fear and insecurity. You paddled right around the bay of giving up. You even turned turtle and let embarrassment flow right over you. Now that you're out here with all those teeth showing, let's really have some fun.

Let's take off on a four-footer, pop-up early, and pull off a pretty bottom turn. Let's careen down the face the wave, wind in our hair, as jealous

the face or the unbroken part of a wave is what a ramp is to skateboarders

heads turn to see us. We could even share a wave, make silly faces, and giggle as we kick out. This is surfing, and it's all for us.

We've reached a place where there's no turning back. We've been bitten by the bug. We watch waves like bookies watch horses. We know tides like moms know feeding schedules. We know which Sex Wax® (a brand of surf wax) gets

us the best sticky bumps and which point break goes off on a south swell. There's salt in our veins and seaweed in our teeth. We were the first ones to get wet on that foggy morning when the sets rolled in like pancakes, lined up like first-day-of-school notebook paper—clean like ice and pretty like porcelain. Yes, we want it more than they do.

To experience the thrills of surfing, take a good look at this chapter. This is the chapter that should help you improve enough to find the real joy in surfing.

CATCHING FACE

The face of the wave is the nut inside the shell. It's the good stuff, the thing we really want after cracking through all the mess and confusion. The face, or the unbroken part of a wave, is what a ramp is to skateboarders. It's where you ride and create your line on the wave. It is your jazz solo, an improvisational painting on a three-second canvas. It's fleeting, yet so satisfying.

It does take quite a bit of practice to catch and ride the face of a wave. In order to do it, try these steps.

Be in the sweet spot

Ever watch a great surfer when she's not on a wave? She's usually the one paddling by you with that big grin on after she's ridden a pretty left. Great surfers know where to be at any given moment. Years of surfing have honed their homing beacons. They can judge, by the placement of the lineup, their position on the coast; they know, by the intuition in their hearts, where to be at any given moment to maximize their ability to catch good waves. Sometimes this *wave knowledge* is very conscious, and sometimes it's subconscious.

Learn from them through observation and osmosis. Watch where they're going and when they're going there. Find a friend who's an accomplished surfer and follow her around while asking questions. "Why did you paddle inside that guy and a few feet farther out than him?" "How come you keep paddling south?" You might get answers like this: "The set waves are breaking left, starting from about here. In order to catch one of these waves, you've gotta be closest to the peak, which means I have to paddle to the inside of that guy to have priority on the wave." Or, "I keep paddling south because the rip current is pulling us north. Look at our position compared to the lifeguard tower. We used to be right in front of it . . ."

Being in the right place at the right time is a big part of surfing. In order to catch face, you're going to have to put yourself right where the waves form and build steepness. Watch lots of waves and ask questions—one day it will become second nature.

This is the kind of surfing that made Mary Osborne the longboard winner of the MTV *Surf Girls* reality show.

Mary Bagalso, carving beautiful turns on the face of the wave.

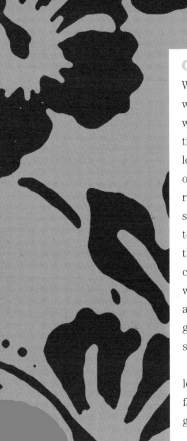

Choose an open wave

Wave selection is also crucial in surfing. Not every wave is going to have an open, rideable face. Some waves *wall-up* and then crash, all at the same time. When choosing a wave, you're going to be looking for one that has a *peak* (the highest point of a wave) and a *shoulder* (the steep area to the right or left of the peak). A good shoulder has steepness for several yards and then starts to flatten out. This flatter section is the part of the wave that will start to steepen as the wave breaks successively down the line. This is ultimately what we want—a wave that breaks successively instead of all at once. As you're choosing a wave, it's also a good idea to look around and see if there are other surfers trying to catch the same wave.

If you're a goofy-foot, riding a wave toward the left is called riding *frontside*—because you are facing the wall of the wave as you're riding. As a goofy-foot, when you ride toward the right, your

in the last moments before you catch a wave, make sure you have the right-of-way

back is facing the wave and you are riding *backside*. For a regular-footer, it's vice versa (a left is backside, a right is frontside). Our ultimate goal is to make you comfortable riding in both directions. However, as a beginner, you may find it easier to

start by catching and riding frontside waves. It's generally considered easier to ride frontside because it's easier to see the wave in front of you as you're riding it. When you're riding backside, you have to look over your shoulder to be able to see the wave behind you.

Line yourself up

Once you're in the right spot and you've chosen the right wave, turn your board quickly (remember, timing is everything) to get in position for the wave. Ask yourself, "Is this wave a right or a left?" Remember that it's easier to start by catching waves that will be frontside for your particular stance. Then point your board at a slight angle in the direction you've decided to go and start paddling like you mean it.

Paddle deep, then fast

Remember our section on paddling? Take a second to make your body like an arrow—properly positioned from side to side and front to back. Start with a few deep and slow paddles (to get your momentum going), and then begin quickening your paddle as the wave approaches. Your job is to paddle at a slight angle and get yourself "into" the wave in the direction that it's going.

Check for other surfers

In the last moments before you catch a wave, make sure you have the right-of-way. Look to the left and right to make sure no one is paddling or

Notice how Mary pops up early, before the wave has broken. This will position her to be standing and in control as she moves down the face of the wave.

board should be moving diagonally down the face of the wave toward the right or left. As you're dropping in, slowly rise from the crouching position to a ready position (knees slightly bent, feet shoulder-width apart, hands facing forward). Now you're ready to keep it moving. If the wave has an open face and you've dropped in with good timing, you should be riding the face!

Follow the line

Breathe and relax. This is what it's all about. As you're riding, look around to make sure there are no other surfers in your path. Stay in your ready stance and ride sideways down the line of the wave as it breaks behind you.

Smile a big smile, because you've done something that you'll remember for a long time to come!

HOW TO STEER THE DARN THING

Unfortunately, this thing does not have a steering wheel. No rudder, no handlebars, and no leash. Unless you train it to follow your lead, this overgrown puppy is going wherever it wants to go.

It's interesting to note that most surfers were never *taught* how to turn. Most of us just learned through trial and error—lots of it! As a result, many of us are not conscious of the methods we use for turning. So, what you're getting here is a bit of extra information that will make your learning curve steeper than ours. The words here may seem meaningless to you unless you've tried it.

has already stood up on the wave. If someone is paddling closer to the peak/whitewater, or has already stood up, you must pull out of the wave. Remember the rules of surfing etiquette we discussed in Chapter 5. Also, look ahead to make sure no one is paddling right in front of you.

Pop up and drop in

As soon as you feel the wave moving you (timing is everything), pop up to your feet in one graceful motion. In order to ride the face successfully, you need to be up onto your feet before you've reached the bottom half of the wave (top to bottom). Start your stance in a fairly low, crouching position to give yourself balance as you're moving down the steepest part of the wave. Since you pointed your board at an angle when you were paddling, your

Turning is something that you really can't learn from reading. The best way to learn is to go out there and try it over and over again.

Despite the complex physics involved, there are essentially two ways to turn a surfboard when it's in motion on a wave: by using the *rails* (edges) or by *pivoting*. Surfers use both—sometimes simultaneously, and sometimes independently.

Using the rails to turn means that the surfer is essentially leaning toward one edge of the board to cause a turn. If you lean on the right edge of a board, for example, the left edge of the board will lift up ever so slightly. This left edge will have less friction in the water and will move more quickly than the right edge. Imagine a car when the left wheel is being powered faster than the right wheel. That car will turn to the right. It's the same basic concept on a surfboard.

Using the rails (or edges) to make turns on a longboard can be quite challenging and sometimes ineffective. A longboard is big, so it has a lot of weight (momentum) moving in a forward direction. It would take a lot of leaning to turn something with that much forward motion. Sometimes you'll see a surfer try to lean the board on edge to turn it—and they lean so much they fall over. The longboard keeps going straight, just the way it wanted to.

Another way to turn a longboard is to pivot it. Think of the board as a teeter-totter. If you stand on one end of a teeter-totter, the other end goes up. On a longboard, if you place your feet toward

Notice how Mary Bagalso uses the board's rail, its tail, and her body to pull off this pretty "cutback" turn.

the back of the board, you can lift the nose slightly and direct it in the direction you want to go.

To do a pivot turn, place both feet near the tail of the board (toes facing either to the left or right rail, depending on your stance). Your back foot will be the pivot point and your forward foot will be the guiding foot. Lean backward slightly and keep your back foot steady as you pull the board to the right or left with your front foot. If you've ever ridden a skateboard, it's essentially the same maneuver as stepping on the tail and pivoting the board back and forth. In fact, it's a good idea to practice the mechanics of the maneuver at home on a skateboard.

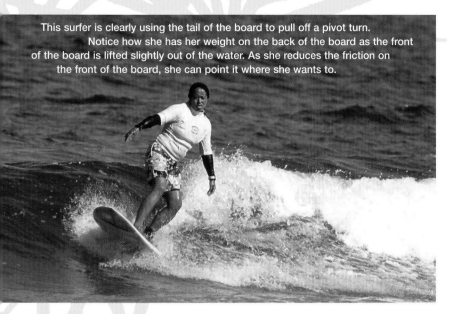

This surfer is clearly using the tail of the board to pull off a pivot turn. Notice how she has her weight on the back of the board as the front of the board is lifted slightly out of the water. As she reduces the friction on the front of the board, she can point it where she wants to.

One of the key turns that you should practice is the *bottom turn*. Bottom turns can help you get to the right section or get out of a wave that is closing out. This turn is just what it sounds like: a turn made at the bottom, or trough, of a wave. To carry out a bottom turn, drop in somewhat diagonally down the face of the wave. As you get to the bottom, lean your body in toward the face of the wave as you place most of your weight on your back foot. You should feel the tail of your board digging into the water as the nose of your board begins moving back up the face of the wave. A great bottom turn can feel so good that—well, we shouldn't get explicit . . . But it's a great feeling!

Now that you understand how you can turn a surfboard, go out there and try it. Use the edge method and the pivot method together. Practice turning with your toe edge and your heel edge. Try pivoting to the left and to the right. One day you'll be pulling off pretty bottom turns and wicked cutbacks!

ELEMENTS OF STYLE: HOW TO LOOK FABULOUS ON A WAVE

Along with feeling great, you might as well *look* great while you're on a wave. The way you stand, hold your arms, turn, and paddle are all elements of your style. Focusing on your style not only improves how you look aesthetically; it also improves your surfing overall.

Can you imagine what it would be like to judge a surf contest? There are no goals or baskets to help you keep score. There are no guidelines or degrees of difficulty that would help judge one surfer's ride against another's. The essential reason why surfing is so hard to judge is because surfing is both sport and art. What a surfer does on a wave and how she does it is essentially a matter of how she expresses herself. Does she decide to do a quick bottom turn and hit the lip, or will she tuck into the barrel and pull off a cutback? Is her stance crouched with her arms in front of her, or is she riding mostly upright with her knees slightly bent in a show of relaxed grace? The line she paints on the wave and the way she holds her body are all expressions of the surfing art. As with traditional art forms, who's to say whether a Georgia O'Keeffe painting is better than a Modigliani?

As with most of the advice we've given you, there are some differences between style on a longboard and style on a shortboard. Each type of board has its cultural norms and stylistic traditions. In the tradition of longboarding, the highest goal is relaxed grace.

Longboard style

The ultimate longboarder looks totally at ease on the wave and in control of her destiny. She uses minimum effort to achieve maximum results. Her body is mostly upright, her feet not too far apart, and she knows how to dance the board. This dancing on the board—known as *cross-stepping*—is when a longboarder travels up and down the board by walking sideways, with one foot crossing over the other as she moves her way to the nose of the board. Watch some longboarding videos and you'll see this graceful walk.

The ultimate end to a pretty cross-walk is to hang ten (literally, hanging ten toes over the nose). Hanging ten—or even its cousin, the cheater-five (five toes on the nose)—are the ultimate tricks in longboarding. The thing about hanging ten is that it seems totally impossible. How can one stand on the end of a 9½-foot board and not have the nose sink into the water? It's a fabulous feat of physics that just does not seem to make sense. This is the strange magic we call surfing.

Having your legs spread wide apart like this is actually not good for balance, or for style . . .

Notice the upright stance, feet shoulder-width apart, and the relaxed grace of Mary Bagalso.

interview:

Mary Bagalso

ICU nurse/pro surfer, age thirty-one
Oceanside, California

For a New Jersey girl who lives in Southern California, Mary has a lot of aloha. A pro surfer and nurse, she tells us how to deal with territorial males, what she does on her vacations, and about her experience with the "killer palm tree."

What is the purpose of surfing? For me, it's about being alive. Even when I'm not in the water, I'm thinking about it.

What is your life like as a pro surfer? For me it's just living. The difference is just that I get paid to surf—that's the only thing that makes someone a pro. And that's when the pressure comes on. You either have to do well in contests, or you have to produce the photo, the video, or write the article to make things happen as a pro. Those are some of the hard parts, but they're also some of the fun parts. You know, you challenge yourself every day, whether it's working to make a better turn, trying to trim a board better, or just trying to communicate with your body and the board to be one in the ocean. To feel that all the time is difficult.

It's work, but it's probably my most enjoyable work. You know, it's better than going to the hospital and pumping on someone's chest just to get them to come back again.

I do at least ten contests a year because I've always been a competitor. And even if you know you're not going to be a pro, I think entering contests is great because it forces you into another mindset, where you will discover something new about yourself. I thrived off that for many years. You know you have to perform within that fifteen-minute block of time.

But you don't have to be a pro surfer to enter; you can enter amateur contests. And you'll be amazed at what you'll learn about yourself in that fifteen minutes with your heart pounding [laughter]. . . . You're so nervous!

I'm not saying everyone should go out and do a contest, but if you want to get better, you should think about it.

What have you learned about yourself in pro surfing? I learned that I can't force things . . . I can't just make it happen because I want the wave to do it. Sometimes Mother Nature will deal her cards, and you have no choice. I also learned that you can't win them all. You can win most, you can try hard—but every day can't always be yours! That was a hard thing for me, because I thought hard work equals success equals you have to win. But no. That's not really the formula. It's hard work *can* equal success, but you take some of the losses. You take it and you grow from it . . . If you let it get to you, you're just gonna bury yourself in the whitewash . . .

You can't take it seriously, you know. You're still breathing, you're still alive. At least you can go surf [laughter]. Things could be a lot worse!

But when I tried the longboard, we just fit. You know when you see something and you want to eat it and it tastes good? Well, that's how it was for me. I tried a longboard and it was my candy! [laughter] It was instant.

Have you dealt with much sexism out in the water? Absolutely. I've had many different kinds of experiences with it. You know, when you're wearing a bikini and a guy is just being a guy . . . and then there's the guy who doesn't think you can surf and has to make fun of you. Then there's the guy who admires you for how well you surf, and the girl whose boyfriend's watching you . . . [laughter] So there are many instances of sexism in the water. But for the most part in the last few years, the guys are starting to warm up to women being in the water. If anything, it diffuses the testosterone trip.

When were you the most afraid? Oh, when I almost drowned in Hawaii! [laughter] The day started out small, you know, it was like five feet and I was surfing in the Waimea area. I was surfing inside pinballs [a surf break], and then four hours later I'm surfing triple, quadruple overhead surf [waves that are four times taller than you] and I'm pinned down for like a minute underwater, after

being hit by a twenty-foot-plus wave. And I'm thinking, "Oh my God, I'm gonna drown," and actually having my body feel so weak, that I literally blacked out. And to know that it could be my last day. And I could feel my lungs get heavy and could feel all the water and emotion throwing me in so many directions that I didn't know which way was up.

I made it down the face of the wave, but then the offshore wind caught under my board and threw me. And then the lip of the wave came right on top of me and I went tumbling. And I got tumbled for a while. When I finally got up for air, like just when my lips touched the air, another wave hit me.

Thank God my leash didn't break, but when I took it out, it was like twenty-five feet long! [A longboard leash is usually about nine to ten feet long. Mary's leash was stretched by the force of the wave.] I finally got my board and I saw another three waves on the horizon. And I don't think I've ever paddled so hard. My lungs were burning and my body was aching but I had to go past the pain. Forget pain, fear is my companion here. Fear is gonna get me out of this situation!

That's the most afraid I've ever been. But there was another time . . . in the Mentawi Islands where they have this right-hand point break that has this inside section called The Surgeon's Table, because the reef has cut many people open . . . Well, I took off on one wave and I didn't make it. But once I got to the

bottom I saw a palm tree—a palm frond, like a really big one—coming down the face of the wave at me, and it almost hit me. And then I broke my toe on that wave, because my leash got stuck in my foot and my toe got ripped the other way. I was sure that it was cut off, but it was just broken. So I had to jam it back the other way, or else it was just over.

It was a ten- to twelve-foot face in Indonesia, at a surf break called Hollow Trees. Yeah, this isn't a wave you mess around with. You don't flirt with it; you don't tickle that wave [laughter]. That wave will eat you!

After you experience something like that, do you go in and take a rest, or do you just go right back out for another one? I have to go back out, because if I don't, I'll probably never go back out. It hurt like heck after I broke my toe, but I caught a couple more and then I went back in. I just needed to get it out of my system. I don't want to be one of those people who says, "I shoulda, I woulda, I coulda . . ." If I don't at least try, it will bother me for the rest of my life.

If you had children, what would you teach them about surfing? First, to respect the ocean. Never underestimate her. Treat the ocean with respect, because we might not have it if we don't keep it clean. You know, I'd never force it on them. It's got to come on their own time.

Mary O, going for a classic cheater-five . . .

Shortboard style

Our intrepid shortboarder has an entirely different aesthetic in mind. Her highest desire is to ride the wave like it's a skateboard ramp. She can make quick sharp turns, hit the lip, catch air, and tuck into the gorgeous green room of a tubing wave. A shortboard is about speed and radical maneuvers—and the shortboarder aims to push the limits of a wave and use it as her playground.

As you progress, watch other surfers in the water and in surf videos. Notice the minutiae. Notice how they hold their arms, where they place their feet, and what maneuvers they make while they're on the wave. Focus on one element of surfing, such as where you hold your arms, the width of your stance, or learning how to cross-step. Try to improve that element on every wave you catch that week.

There's no reason to look like anyone else out there. However, paying attention to your style will ultimately help you refine your wave riding and can add an entirely new level of fun to the sport.

HOW TO MAKE BANTER OUT ON THE HIGH SEAS

We have an issue with surfers these days. It seems more often than not, in California at least, surfers are not talking to each other much. It used to be that you'd paddle out, greet surfers in the lineup, get caught up with old friends, hoot and holler for folks who got great rides, make jokes, discuss surf forecasts (usually to be taken with a grain of sea salt), and generally have a good time in the water. Nowadays you encounter these surfers who have that steely-eyed glare, eyes transfixed on the ocean, and not much of a smile to be found. Hey folks, do you remember that surfing is supposed to be fun?

Yes, surfing can be a very meditative and solitary sport. For some, that is exactly what they are seeking. Nonetheless, let's make surfing fun again.

We know we're not supposed to make broad general statements, but I think on the whole, surfers are a good and friendly tribe. The ocean has a tendency to produce and nurture goodness. As you're out there on the high seas, talk to your fellow surfers. You don't have to know all the lingo. In fact, in many surfing cultures there's nothing worse than a poser who tries to use lingo to establish himself as a veteran. Read surf magazines and watch surf videos to understand the terms. Ask about the conditions, be humble and ask for advice, make jokes. Most surfers would welcome the opportunity to pass on some of their knowledge and connect with the other surfers out there. Sometimes the presence of women out in the water cools down the intensity of the testosterone—and people start chatting and having fun. This is a good thing. If you go out to a particular surf break regularly, you'll start to know the regulars and they'll start to know you. This can only help you develop as a surfer.

Mary's Tips

So you have made it through several wipeouts, bruises on strange areas of your body, and continuous evenings with water dripping out of your nose—and you still want to learn more. This is great! You may feel like a kid in a candy store every time you check the surf; you are stoked to be in the water, and now you have the surf bug in you forever. Learning all the basics is extremely hard work, but don't give up yet; learning advanced techniques takes time and dedication as well. Here are seven tips to help you bridge the gap from beginner to advanced surfer.

1. Making time

Just like any other physical activity, the only way you will get better is by practicing. The most glorious things about surfing are that no two sessions will ever be alike, a wave will never break the same, and Mother Nature is constantly changing. It's simple: the more you practice, the better you become.

I hate to say it, but there is life beyond surfing. Many surfers have jobs, kids, and a family to look after. Some of us may have more time than others to surf—but the reality is, there is always a way to make room. Make time in your busy schedules to go out and catch a few waves. Maybe it's as simple as waking up earlier before school or work, or finishing daily assignments earlier than usual. Make time to surf! The more you go, the more comfortable and better you will become.

If you live far away from the ocean, try to maintain that stoked feeling by watching surf videos, practicing pop-ups, reading books and magazines, and dreaming of your next vacation.

2. Eyes wide open

Surfing is a very individual sport. No one is telling you when to go, where to line up, when to paddle and stand up—except that little voice in your head. The best way to advance to a new level is by watching other surfers and surfing with friends who have a bit more experience. Before you paddle out to a new spot, take a few moments on the beach to observe where the surfers are sitting and where the waves are breaking. Ask questions from surfing friends who have more experience. Once you're out in the lineup at a new spot, let a few waves go by and watch which way surfers are going: right, left, or both? Remember to keep your eyes open at all times and be aware of what is going on around you.

3. Return to your center

Surfing is a meditation. One of surfing's greatest lessons is about staying calm amidst the chaos. Remember to breathe and to visualize success on each wave. If your mind is saying, "I'm gonna fall. What if I miss the wave? My feet are going to slip off . . ." then that's probably what will happen. Visualize your smooth and powerful paddle, your quick and easy pop-up, your nice bottom turn. Soon this will become a reality. Sometimes we see surfers with a contorted face as they try to catch a wave— the kind of face one might put on for a battle. Surfing is about

oneness with the ocean, not about battling it. So remember to return to your center, breathe, and find your synergy.

4. Equipment

This may sound crazy, but I watched six-time world champion Kelly Slater ride waves on a table top, a suitcase, and an old wooden sled. An excellent surfer can surf almost anything. Nonetheless, it helps to try different surfboards to determine what your preferences may be. Sometimes waves are extremely small or enormously large, and having a variety—a quiver—of surfboards will help you adapt to diverse waves. Trying different surfboards will only make you a well-rounded surfer.

5. Fitness

I'm not a gym person, but I make up for it with other physical activity. Any type of strength training that correlates with surfing is beneficial. For example: skateboarding, snowboarding, biking, running, volleyball, swimming, paddle boarding, yoga, stretching, etc. It is rare that you see a very unfit surfer—and staying active is a huge part of the surfing lifestyle. Try the exercises in Chapter 7—and overall, just try to stay healthy and happy.

6. Get Visual

Video yourself

Grab a friend, get a video recorder, and head to the beach. One of the best ways to improve your surfing style is by watching and critiquing yourself on video. The first time I saw myself on tape I was horrified, and hated my style. I was able to see what I did wrong on a wave, why I fell, and how I could change. It may be scary and a shock to see yourself at first—but trust me, it will only make you improve faster.

Mary's tips

Women of all ages surf.

Study magazines and surf movies

Surf magazines are a great way to pick up tips. They are filled with so much useful information, such as advice on riding waves, choosing equipment, fitness, and traveling. Many of your curiosities may be answered simply by reading a surf magazine. Another great way to improve your style, tricks, and knowledge is by watching surf movies. Watching the top professionals can get you to a better understanding and a higher level. Try to notice little things, like where they position their feet and what decisions they make on a wave.

7. Fun

As Surf Diva Surf School says, "The best surfer in the water is the one having the most fun." Surfing is all about the joy of catching waves and the unbelievable and desirable feeling you get from it! Sometimes you see surfers out in the water who rarely crack a smile. What's the point of surfing if you're not having fun? Delight in your wipeouts, be gentle with yourself, and remember to return to your center. Make the most of your surfing experiences and enjoy every moment Mother Nature gives you.

Meditation at Las Olas Surf Safaris in Mexico.

Las Olas stories

By Bev Sanders, founder, Las Olas Surf Safaris for Women

Another great way to learn surfing is to get away for a premier surfing vacation with companies like Las Olas Surf Safaris. Women's surf safaris like these offer fabulous amenities like organic food, elegant accommodations, and massages. The stories below attest to how transformational this combination can be. Why not pamper yourself in the process of learning how to surf?

Pre-beach instruction at Las Olas Surf Safaris in Mexico.

If I was told that I would redirect my entire life because of a single experience, I would have ignored the idea. I had heard of this happening to other people, but I never thought much about it or connected the phenomenon to my world. I've always felt these types of experiences either inspired someone to move in a direction they were already moving toward—or the experience was so earth-shattering it forced them to change.

But that was before I learned to surf.

I would never have expected an activity so obvious, so typical, would get under my skin—but surfing my first waves gave me a new sense of clarity. It reawakened the sure-footed confidence that helped me break from my two-decade career as cofounder and marketing director of a successful snowboard company. Playing in the waves, I reconnected to that part of myself that was independent, joyful, and free. By the end of the year, I knew exactly what I wanted to do with the next chapter in my life. I would share my new sense of freedom by teaching surfing: I would make girls out of women.

Launched in 1997, Las Olas Surf Safaris set the standard for women's destination surf schools. Yoga, oceanside villas, healthful meals, massage, and a host of other activities reconnected us to ourselves and our community. The safaris offered women of all ages the chance to learn and enjoy surfing in a relaxed, noncompetitive environment.

For many guests at Las Olas, a typical day starts out with a surf-specific yoga session—carefully chosen to gently stretch the muscles used during surfing and to get them ready to paddle out again.

Warmth, women, and waves.
What a great combination!

After a rejuvenating breakfast with local mangoes and other fresh tropical fruit, the "girls" review the daily schedule to plan their day. Some will head right out for the break, some will keep an appointment for a relaxing full-body massage, and some will take time to enjoy this friendly fishing village before heading out to surf in a later session.

Throughout the afternoon, itineraries include a second surf session, a siesta, or a cerveza and fresh guacamole at a surfside café. And of course, there's the ongoing beach party of constantly changing instructors and guests who cheer for the girls out in the water and learn by discussing the break and the lineup.

Again and again, I hear stories from our alumnae of how the Las Olas experience has spilled into their lives and the positive energy that returns home with them. It stirs our intuition about connectivity, life, and what's truly important. The following stories are from real women who have attended Las Olas. In their own words, they reveal their apprehension about learning how to surf, and they share their victories. For many, the experience changed their connection with themselves, the ocean, and the world around them.

"I think I am probably the story of the nonathlete who, without realizing it, became one. First, the decision to learn to surf became one of the steps in ending a long, but unhappy, marriage and finding my own independence. I was never a swimmer. One day at the beach with my now ex-husband, I saw a sixteen-year-old girl out on a longboard with her father beside her. I watched her and said, 'I want to learn how to do that.' The response I heard was, 'Are you kidding? Maybe you should think about a boogie board. You can't do that.'

"In a moment of total clarity, I knew two things: one, I would learn to surf no matter what. And two, I couldn't stay with someone who had time and time again shown me that he had no belief in me. I went out the next weekend and bought a board, and went right out into rough surf. Scared me to death, and bruised every part of my body. It was my mother who found the Las Olas ad and said to me, 'This is what you need.' And that is what I did—I was on one of the first safaris. And I didn't do that well. I actually cried on Izzy's shoulder, I was so terrified of the water. But I was learning. Not one to give up, I have kept at it, learning the ocean and learning about me. Overcoming fear in life and in the water, I have since returned to Las Olas two more times, always learning something new. And look at me now!"

Las Olas Surf Safaris pampers its guests with massage, yoga, and organic food.

"Being a native New Yorker, the ocean was never in my backyard; it was an experience I had maybe once or twice a summer. I truly learned the virtues of patience and communing with nature. By the end of the trip I was catching waves. Now, I remind myself on a daily basis how to be patient and work with nature, not against it."

Central Mexico offers beautiful surroundings for a relaxing surfing vacation.

"My decision to finally take my first surfing lesson in Waikiki two years ago was the initial step in emerging from the predictable, stable, risk-averse lifestyle—or lifeless style—imposed by our culture. That lesson climaxed with a successful ride on my third attempt, and the thrill and sense of pride from that moment reawakened distant memories of the twenty-two-year-old adventurer who backpacked from Japan to Egypt via the TransSiberian, sans the benefit of a diplomatic passport. Each subsequent surfing adventure (especially the wipeouts) taught me that failing is acceptable, but not trying isn't. I have shed my suits and taken bolder steps to seek a career that values adventure and some risk taking."

"My marriage ended, and then surfing changed my life. It made me think, 'Why not?!' So why not live three months a year in another country? (Near some good waves, of course!) I'm forty-two, I have three kids, two businesses, and one life—and I intend to live it to the fullest! 'Today is a gift; that's why it's called the present.'"

"In addition to it being one of the most incredible vacations I ever had—and I don't even like group trips!—I quit my corporate job and am back in school for writing, in large part because of my surfing experience."

"Within the course of a month, I lost both my job and my boyfriend—who I thought I was going to marry. This was a time of great upheaval and self-examination. When I stood up on the board for the first time, an epiphany occurred. With the backdrop of the other women whooping and clapping, I knew I could do anything, and the rest of humanity wanted me to be a success! My life was going to be just fine."

"Yesterday I surfed my first double overhead wave. I dropped down that glassy face with a terror-turned-thrill that no one can ever teach you. Yet, if you hear that Las Olas encouragement, you'll discover this despite your fear. Since I've completed my surf camps in Mexico, I've finished a novel and begun another. I've been encouraged and encouraged others. I've wiped out and fought my way back into the lineup from a rough inside. Surfing wakes you up to yourself, the community, and the Earth. Corny sounding, I know, but true. You paddle out there and tell me it's not."

"We found ourselves at Las Olas Surf Safaris for Women. We were new to surfing as well as each other, but the power of sisterhood lifted and encouraged us, helped us stand, literally, to that glorious position of achievement on the surfboard. We did it! Our individuality is powerful, but together, our sisterhood speaks volumes."

my surgery, I need you to leave as much of my pectoralis major there as possible, so I can still have my chest muscles because those are really important for pushing up on the board."

My experience with cancer was made more bearable because I knew that I wanted to go out into the ocean as soon as I possibly could, and that remained my dream and my goal. The ocean is so much a passion in my life that it really helped me to heal, to have the right attitude for healing.

What do you remember about Rell Sunn? She was incredibly warm, incredibly giving and graceful. She was an absolutely amazing woman who lived for many, many years with metastatic breast cancer. And she never let it ruin her day, ever.

You know, we all know we're going to die someday; we just don't know when it is. As she went through her life, she really chose to go through it in the water, with grace, not really knowing when her end was going to be. But, man, she really lived life to the fullest. She was a tremendous example for me.

Rell had grace in living and she even had grace in dying. If I go out, let me go out with as much gracefulness as I can.

Is there a connection for you between surfing and spirituality? Completely. It's the same. It is absolutely the same. You know, people say, "Oh, I have to go to church on Sunday . . ." and I think, Well, I need to go to the ocean today.

To me the god that lives inside all of us is a level of energy. The energy that is the light of the best person that you can ever be. The ocean provides that energy without any human involvement. It just *is*. And you can feel the energy—the energy of the wave or of the storm, or the flat, glassy, incredible water. That is the ultimate spirituality without human form. I feel it on a very deep level. But it's hard to describe. It's a meditation and it's church-like. It's right there.

What advice do you have for women who want to make surfing a part of their lives? If you want to make it part of your life, bring it in, bit by bit. You may end up changing your entire life, so you can be around, near, in the ocean. But if you don't check in to that, then you'll never know. Don't be frustrated by being a beginner. Let that be OK for you. Let yourself be egoless. Actually, take your ego out of it and enjoy.

If you need to make changes in your life, do it. See how you can set your life up differently. Maybe you're moving too quickly and you need to slow down.

If you're afraid, find out what you're afraid of. Maybe you're going to have to deal with what you're afraid of before you go out in the water. But make sure you deal with it, or it will come out. You know, you'll hesitate, or you'll fall, you'll do something that will remind you that you have more things to deal with. But surfing will help you to do that. Approach your fear.

The bottom line is that it ends up helping you with all the other areas of your life, whether [that is] raising your children or having a better relationship with your partner—whatever that is for you . . .

You know, "Go for it!" [laughter] But I hate that phrase . . . It's about keeping your eyes open and seeing what surfing can be for you.

* Zeuf and her husband Frosty work with an organization called Ride A Wave, whose mission it is "To give everyone the chance to experience the thrill of riding a wave, whether they are physically, economically, or developmentally challenged." For more information, go to www.rideawave.org.

Riding the New York City subway and riding a wave

By Laura Marie Thompson, theater artist/high school teacher, New York, New York

I came to a realization—that riding the New York City subway is distinctly parallel to riding a wave.

- Both require, excite, and promote faith.
- Both require balance—and with your feet apart about shoulder-width, you can find your stance.
- It's more fun and even safe when you make eye contact with the other riders.
- Both transcend language.
- At certain times of the day, it can be so crowded that hostility emerges.
- The implicit danger is such that each or any ride could be your last.
- Sexism often prevails and demands to be challenged.
- Both are better with humor and humility.
- Watching a sunset as you await a ride adds to the sublime beauty of it all.
- Both can be extremely hot or extremely cold.
- It's more fun when shared with those you love.
- There are many sophisticated, crucial, and unwritten rules and expectations of etiquette.
- These rules/expectations are sometimes violated.
- It's more than too bad that trash is sometimes about.
- The experience is sometimes done in silence, sometimes with fretless chatter, and sometimes deep thoughts are shared.
- If you're in a bad mood, it's not nice to take it out on others on the ride.
- People can be so territorial.
- Getting on the ride, even to the ride, can be difficult physically and spiritually.
- You might wait a long time for a ride.
- You might feel exhausted after a day of it.
- Trusting a gut feeling can save your life.
- I am grateful to experience both in this life.

CHAPTER 7

SURF FITNESS

By Janine Daley, MS Exercise Physiology, ACE (American Council on Exercise) Certified Personal Trainer, Medical Exercise Specialist, Certified Health Promotion Director (Cooper Institute), Advanced Fitness Specialist (Cooper Institute).

Women are highly suited for the sport of surfing. In general, our bodies are more flexible than men's. In addition, our strength-to-body weight ratio can at times be an advantage. Women present a smaller profile in the wind (as we paddle out on our surfboards). We have less weight and musculature, so we tend to be more fluid in our movements.

However, if we don't condition our bodies, we won't be able to reap the benefits of our natural endowment. Our level of fitness can greatly impact how much fun we have in surfing. Surfing tests our cardiovascular fitness along with all the muscles needed for paddling. The better shape we're in, the more waves we'll be able to catch, and the more fun we'll have out in the water.

Whether you are a beginning surfer or a seasoned professional, the following exercises will help you achieve your surfing goals. They are designed to get the most bang for your buck without a tremendous time commitment. They are functional exercises that require activation of several muscle groups, rather than focusing on one muscle group over another. Read through the entire chapter before you begin the exercises. If your time is limited, try doing a twenty-minute session using at least one of the exercises from each of the four sections. Once you have mastered the exercises suggested in the chapter, check out the website www.sistersurfer.com for additional information, more advanced exercises, and other exercise options.

The twenty-minute surf workout

Here's a quick twenty-minute surf workout, to get you in shape for surfing. Doing this routine two to three times a week should get you ready to have fun in the water. Try doing two or three sets of each exercise. The exercises are described in detail later in this chapter.

BALANCE
- tree posture
- balancing stick posture

STRENGTH
- push-ups
- pop-ups
- crunches

ENDURANCE
- run, bike, swim, or surf

FLEXIBILITY
- sun salutations

There are four physical considerations when conditioning your body for surfing:

1. **Balance:** to give you the ability to adjust your position quickly to stay upright while the wave is moving beneath you.
2. **Upper body and core strength:** to give you the strength to paddle effectively in order to catch waves and the power to push up to a standing position once a wave is caught.
3. **Endurance:** so you can sustain your paddling while getting through the whitewater en route to the surf line.
4. **Flexibility:** to give you the agility you need to get your feet in the right position for standing on your board, and to prevent injuries.

1. BALANCE

Balance is a key ingredient in surfing since the waves are always changing. The shape of a wave depends on tides, direction of the swell, and wind. One day the waves will be enormous, while the next day they may be small and insignificant. Surfing requires us to be in tune with these changes and able to adapt to them quickly.

Yoga is an excellent discipline to prepare you for surfing. It stimulates your balance receptors, creates flexibility and strength in your joints, and gives you a better awareness of your body in space. Yoga requires us to pay close attention to our bodies, minds, and spirits—and to find our center. It is much easier to balance on a surfboard rocketing through the water if you have this awareness.

Taking a yoga class once in a while, buying a videotape, or practicing at home are all excellent ways to fit yoga into your week. There are even great children's yoga videos if you want to get your children involved.

Here are a few great yoga postures for balance, strength, and stability. When practicing yoga, remember to breathe through each posture. If you find yourself holding your breath, consciously remember to breathe; if you cannot breathe comfortably, come out of the posture and try it again on another day. The posture might be too difficult for you on that day.

Tree posture

Tree posture

1. Stand with your feet firmly rooted to the ground.
2. Bring the bottom of your left foot up to your inner right thigh with your left hand.
3. Place your hands together at your heart level (as in prayer) at the middle of your chest.
4. Raise your hands above your head and then separate and reach them toward the sky (like branches).
5. Try to stay rooted to the ground for a ten-second count, or until your tree feels ready to release the posture.
6. Change legs and repeat.

Balancing stick posture (more advanced)

1. Raise your hands above your head and place them together (as in prayer).
2. Stand on one leg and extend your other leg straight behind you.
3. Point the toe on the extended leg and arch your back slightly on the extended leg side.
4. Focus your gaze four or five feet ahead.
5. Extend out of the base of your spine and pivot your body over the axis point of your hip. The extended leg points backward behind you as your arms point in front of you, straight and strong.
6. Bring your arms out to your sides to balance. Hold for at least ten seconds.
7. Change legs and repeat.

Balancing stick posture

Bow and arrow posture

Bow and arrow posture (most advanced)

1. Place hands together at heart level as in prayer.
2. Feet are firmly rooted to the ground.
3. Place your right arm straight up over your head, pointing to the sky.
4. With your left hand grab your left ankle.
5. Knees are even.
6. Pivot forward at the waist and lower your chest.
7. Arch your back.
8. Extend your arm out in front of you and your foot into your hand.
9. Hold your posture for ten seconds or until you feel ready to come out of the pose.
10. Change legs and repeat.

Bosu ball, wobble, or balance board

Several pieces of exercise equipment have been developed in recent years to stimulate balance, proprioception (awareness of your body in space), and stabilization strength. This equipment can be found in many gyms, in sporting goods stores, and on the Internet. Costs range from $25 to $70 for balance or wobble boards and $124 to $130 for Bosu trainer half-balls. This is very useful equipment, and can add an element of fun to your training. I have included many exercises in this chapter that utilize this equipment

The following are great balance exercises with the Bosu ball.

One-leg training

Stand on either side of the Bosu ball (the soft half-ball side is easier; the hard side is more advanced) and maintain your balance while standing on one leg. Hint: Keep your eyes focused on a point in front of you.

One-leg medicine ball toss (more advanced)

Do the same as you would the above exercise, but

toss a medicine ball to a friend, at the wall, or in the air—then try to catch it while standing on one leg. Hint: Keep your eyes focused on a point in front of you and watch the ball only with your peripheral vision. Keep in mind that these exercises might take several practice runs before you find success.

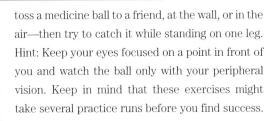

start with the easier exercises and build into the advanced ones

Remember, balance exercises do not require a lot of time. You can do simple things throughout your day to stimulate your balance. Watch children play; you'll see they are always creating ways to challenge themselves. Find new ways to stimulate your balance. Stand on one leg while brushing your teeth, walk on a cement curb like a balance beam, or play with your children (or someone else's children) at the local playground. The children will enjoy the playtime while you gain a better awareness of your body in space.

2. STRENGTH

Upper-body strength is critical for the sport of surfing. It affects your ability to paddle into and out of waves, as well as your ability to pop up to your feet. Because waves don't wait, explosive power is far more important to the surfer than how much weight you can press on the bench press.

The following exercises are designed to help you strengthen your body in a functional way, to prevent overuse injuries, and to increase your explosive power. Start with the easier exercises and build into the advanced ones. Always give yourself at least forty-eight hours between strength-training sessions, for muscular repair. If you are still sore from a previous workout after forty-eight hours, give yourself another day before resuming your training.

Begin by choosing resistance that will enable you to complete between eight and twelve repetitions. Once you are comfortable with many of the exercises, you can add another set so that you are performing two sets of any exercise. Use the first set as a warm-up and the second as your strength builder. Prior to performing any strength-training exercises, include five to ten minutes of warm-up exercises. These can be light cardiovascular exercises like walking, jogging, or rowing. Once your muscles are warm, you can do some light stretches (more about this later in the chapter).

Strengthen for paddling

An important exercise to strengthen for paddling is to paddle. But when it's not feasible to get in the water, the next best thing is to use rubber tubing. This product can be found in most sporting goods stores, catalogs, and on the Internet. The tubing typically costs between $5 and $10. Use the tubing with handles for better grip. The products are made with a flexible rubber material that is easy to take along, wherever you happen to be. The different colors are different levels of resistance, so pick a color tube that challenges you but allows you to finish your stroke. The following exercises will strengthen the muscles of the chest, shoulders, arms, and upper back.

Rubber tubing paddle

This exercise will benefit all the muscles you need for paddling—without getting wet.

1. Encircle a stable column or post with the tubing.
2. Bend over and grip the tubing in both hands.
3. Practice paddling with long strokes.
4. Finish your pull by extending your arms behind you, elbows straight but not locked.

Rubber tubing paddle

Once the stroke is mastered you can increase the speed of the exercise to prepare for fast paddles out of the impact zone (the area where waves break). You can also break the stroke down so that you can practice the first half of the stroke, or the last half—depending on where it is you need to work. Many beginning paddlers rush the stroke and pull out too soon. Remember to extend to full strokes.

Bench dip (beginner)

1. Sit on a bench or another equally sturdy seat.
2. Place your hands on either side of your bottom, gripping the seat. Your feet are flat on the floor.
3. Hold yourself up with your hands as you scoot your bottom off the seat.
4. Use your arm strength to lower yourself (bottom down) toward the floor.
5. Once your elbows reach a 90° angle, raise yourself back up again.

Bench dip

Push-up (beginner)

1. Place your hands just greater than shoulder-width apart.
2. Place your knees on the floor on a towel or pillow.
3. Support your body weight with your hands and knees.
4. Contract your stomach muscles so that your back does not arch or sag (keep your back flat).
5. Inhale and lower your body over your hands.
6. Exhale and push your upper body away from the floor until your arms are straight but elbows are not locked.

Injury Prevention

The following rowing exercises will strengthen your upper and middle back, posterior shoulder muscles, and shoulder girdle in a different way than paddling would. This will help you avoid injuries so you may enjoy surfing for years to come.

Standing with a stretch cord

1. Encircle your stretch cord on a stable object, such as a pole or tree.
2. Place your hands together at heart height.
3. Inhale to oxygenate your muscles.
4. Exhale while pulling the stretch cord out to your sides at shoulder height.
5. Inhale and bring hands together in front of your body.

External/Internal rotation (shoulder)

1. Encircle your stretch cord around a stable post or column.
2. Keep your elbow tucked into your side and at a right angle.
3. Turn your body sideways so that by rotating your arm externally (away from your body), you feel resistance on the stretch cord.
4. Inhale.

Standing with a stretch cord

External/Internal rotation (shoulder)

5. Exhale and rotate arm away from the body.

6. Inhale and return to the starting position.

7. Remain in the same position and change hands. You will now internally rotate the other hand. (You may have to take a step sideways to add enough resistance to the stretch cord.)

8. Internally rotate the other hand, exhaling as you pull the tube and inhaling as you slowly return to your starting position.

9. Turn your body to face the other direction and repeat, using your other hand.

Strengthen for pop-ups

Once you have mastered the paddle and are catching waves, the next step is to be able to get to your feet quickly. The following plyometric exercises train your fast twitch muscles to fire rapidly with power. This will help everything from your pop-ups to your paddles out through the impact zone.

Pop-ups

Pop-ups

1. Lie on your stomach on a hard surface with your hands on either side of your chest (as in a push-up position).

2. Push off the ground with your hands at the same time as you jump up with your feet.

3. Your dominant leg should be between your two hands with your other leg back about two feet. Look down and see which leg is your dominant leg. If it's your right foot, you are goofy-footed; if it's your left foot, you are regular-footed. Regardless of which foot is dominant, try pop-ups on both sides for balancing out musculature.

Plyometric jumping

The following exercise targets gluteus muscles, hamstrings, and quadriceps.

1. Squat down with your knees bent to an almost-90° angle.

2. Jump up as high as you can, extend your arms overhead, and straighten your legs.

3. Land in the starting position, knees bent.

Squats

1. Stand with your feet approximately hip-width apart.

2. Place dumbbells in your hands, or a bar in front of your chest at collarbone level.

3. Inhale as you bend your knees to 90° (your back remains flat, not arched, and your head is lifted).

4. Exhale as you straighten your legs (do not lock out your knees).

Plyometric jumping

Squats

Lower abdominal strength and coordination

Core strength is an important aspect of sports training, and it is the key to surfing as well. Without it you will not be able to get your feet underneath you in a pop-up, adjust your position on a moving board, or take the impact of a crashing wave. When working this area pay close attention to form. Keep your eyes gazing ahead; keep your shoulders, head, and neck in alignment; and keep your mouth closed.

Bosu ball leg lift

1. Sit on the Bosu ball.
2. Exhale and lift your legs up.
3. Inhale and extend your legs back to your starting position. The farther you are able to extend your legs to a straight position, the harder the exercise. If you find yourself arching your back to do this exercise, do not extend your legs fully.
4. Repeat.

Medicine ball leg lifts (more advanced)

1. Lie on the floor on your back and place a medicine ball between your knees.
2. Your hands are on the floor or in the small of your back.
3. Exhale, bend, and lift your legs up to your hips.
4. Inhale and extend your legs out once again. If you find yourself arching your back, this is too difficult for you at this time.
5. Repeat.

Bosu ball leg lift

Medicine ball leg lifts

Exercise ball crunch

1. Lie on your back on an exercise ball with your hands crossed at your chest (beginner), hands extended up behind your head (more advanced), or holding a medicine ball (most advanced).
2. Exhale and curl your body toward your knees.
3. Inhale and return to your start position.

Exercise ball in pike position (more advanced)

This exercise will strengthen core musculature and develop balance.

1. Lie on your stomach on an exercise ball; place your hands at shoulder-width apart or greater.

2. Walk your hands out and simultaneously roll the ball down your legs so that your legs rest on the ball at about your shins.
3. Inhale.
4. Exhale and pike (make an upside-down V with your body), with your bottom to the sky (knees can be bent, which is easier; or straight, which is harder).
5. Hold this position; then roll out of it and back into it.
6. Challenge yourself by rolling the ball from side to side.
7. Lift one leg up to the sky while keeping the other foot on the middle of the ball (do not arch your back).
8. Change legs.

Exercise ball crunch

Exercise ball in pike position

Sun salutation

Your breath should guide the movements.

1. Start with your arms at your heart level in prayer position, feet together.
2. Inhale deeply.
3. Exhale as you sweep your hands downward to your toes and back up above your head.
4. Stretch back to a comfortable backward extension position.
5. Bend at the waist to bring your hands to your feet.
6. Place your hands on the floor (bend your knees if necessary).
7. Completely relax your head; breathe one cycle, allowing your hamstrings (the back of your thighs) to release and open up.
8. Bring your head and eyes up to look at the sky.
9. Bend your knees and step back with your left leg; look up and feel the stretch in the quadriceps (the front of the thigh), the neck, and the shoulders.
10. Bring your right leg back.
11. Bring your bottom up to downward-facing dog (make an upside-down V with your body); feel the stretch in your hamstrings, chest, and shoulders as you stand on your toes.
12. Bring your heels down and feel the stretch in your calves. Bend and stretch both calves one at a time while you bend and straighten your knees.
13. Bring your bottom down so that your body resembles a plank or tabletop.
14. Bring your knees to the floor, swoop your body through your arms so that your chest is facing

forward, the tops of your feet are resting on the floor, and your back is arched (you should resemble a cobra). Stretch your shoulders away from your head.

15. Bring your bottom up to the sky once again (upside-down **V**).

16. Bring your left foot forward until it is between your hands.

17. Look up to the sky.

18. Bring your right foot up to match your left.

19. Straighten your legs while you are still bent over.

20. Place your hands in prayer position and bring your hands out to the sides as you rise up from the bent position to standing. Your hands are in prayer above your head.

21. Bring your hands to your heart level in prayer.

22. Run through this exercise several times, adjusting the speed and stretch as you warm up to the movements.

Tricep stretch

1. Extend your left hand above your head.

2. Bend your left arm at the elbow.

3. Grasp your elbow with your right hand and gently pull your arm up as far as you can comfortably go.

4. Switch arms.

Inner thigh stretch

1. Step your foot out to the side, about three feet.

2. Bend at the waist and touch the floor.

3. Place your hands on both sides of one leg.

4. Gently bend your knee on that side, supporting yourself with your hands, while the other leg is extended. Feel the stretch on the inside of the leg.

5. Change legs.

Tricep stretch

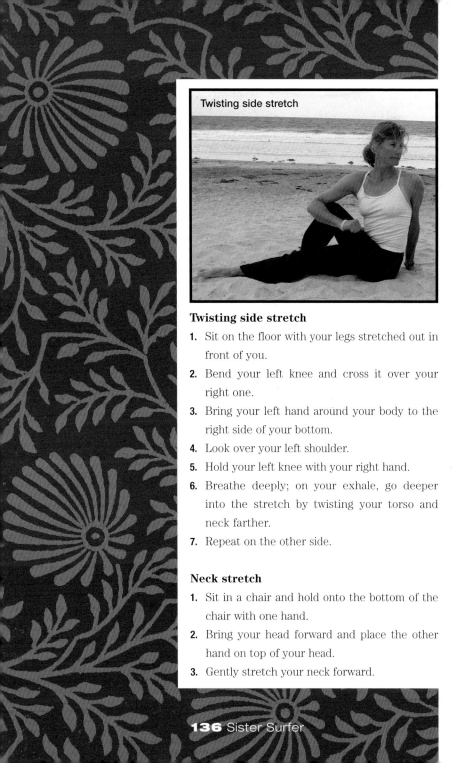

Twisting side stretch

Twisting side stretch

1. Sit on the floor with your legs stretched out in front of you.
2. Bend your left knee and cross it over your right one.
3. Bring your left hand around your body to the right side of your bottom.
4. Look over your left shoulder.
5. Hold your left knee with your right hand.
6. Breathe deeply; on your exhale, go deeper into the stretch by twisting your torso and neck farther.
7. Repeat on the other side.

Neck stretch

1. Sit in a chair and hold onto the bottom of the chair with one hand.
2. Bring your head forward and place the other hand on top of your head.
3. Gently stretch your neck forward.
4. Place your hand on the side of your head and gently stretch to the side.
5. Look ahead and then angle your head to 45°. Place your hand on top of your head and gently stretch your neck forward. Switch sides.
6. Change hands and stretch your neck to the other side.

TAILOR YOUR FITNESS PROGRAM TO YOUR LIFE

Now that you've mastered these exercises, you may want a basic idea of how to design a program for yourself. As a general guideline, if you work all of your body parts, you need to give yourself one day off between your workouts. This means you can probably do the resistance exercises every other day for a maximum of three days per week. However, if you are tight on time, you can gain about 75 percent of the benefits by resistance training two times per week. Aerobic training or endurance training can also be done three days per week, at a minimum.

Focus on the areas you know are weak (i.e., paddling or pop-ups). Do injury prevention exercises once a week. Even if you can only fit in a few sun salutations when you rise, before beginning your busy day, you have done a lot for your balance, flexibility, and strength. When time allows, you can alternate resistance training with aerobic workouts to give yourself something different to do every day. Those who have more time can focus on upper body one day, lower body another—for a

total of five days of exercise per week. Use your aerobic exercise as a warm-up to the resistance training.

You should begin to see results in three weeks. If you stick to your program, you will find that your surfing and fitness will improve on every level. You will feel healthier and look great! Enjoy your new body awareness. Enjoy your ability to run with your children (or someone else's), play in the surf, and feel wonderful again!

interview:

Tais Kintgen and Susana Souza Franca

ages twenty-four and thirty-four
Itacaré, Bahia, Brazil

In the idyllic Brazilian surf town of Itacaré, chickens walk across the cobblestone roads as dreadlocked surfistas wax boards and talk about their surf sessions. This little Hawaii in Brazil is a paradise. Tais and Susana spoke to us about their relationship with surfing.

How do you feel about the water?
Tais: I feel at peace with myself. It is a moment that I relax, a moment I am reflecting on my life, a moment that all my adrenaline and all my feelings are going to the water. When I lived with my grandparents in São Paulo, I was a little child and there was a dog. He was a cocker spaniel, and he liked the water very much, so he jumped together with us in the pool. I was swimming with him and he brought me with him. My grandfather always liked the water very much and he always signed me up for swimming classes. If I learned how to swim back alone, like the dog, I won an ice cream!

When did you learn how to surf?
Tais: I started to surf a little while ago, more or less a few years with an actual surfboard. I surfed for many years on a boogie board, one they sell here in Brazil called Alligator, since I was six years old. But now with the surfboard, it is more difficult.

What was it like for you to learn how to surf? *Susana:* Surfing is very difficult. You must be with a good mind before you get physical, but it is about balance. I am learning; sometimes I get up on the board, but some days I can't. You are paddling, paddling the wave, and it is faster than you—but you must try, persist. How much you persist is how much you will get better. You will feel safer, stronger, and determined—so you are getting to be better. This is what I think.

Were you accepted by men in the water? *Tais:* There are men who give support, some men go to surf and they say, "Go there and take that wave." But others are prejudiced. They say things like, "You shouldn't learn here. There is a right beach for you to learn to surf; go to that other beach."

Some years ago, there was a little discrimination regarding women surfers, but today we are getting all the space—not only in the surf, but in everything. There is good marketing, so today there isn't reason to discriminate: the taboo that women can't surf is finished. Today there are bricklayer women [who] build houses, so I think the women can go there and do it. This thing about machismo, that a man is powerful, is over—because the

Itacaré, Brazil—a surfer's paradise.

woman is doing the same things they are. Now we are the same, brothers and sisters of soul and of surf.

Susana: There isn't much discrimination, but there is a little discrimination with women's competitions. We need more incentive, more support, more sponsorships for women surfers. But we do have women's surf magazines already.

What fears do you have about surfing? *Tais:* I am afraid of the fins, because injuries can happen; you must take care because the fin can hurt your face. There are hard hurts—you can break your foot, get hurt a lot—but you should always take care.

You can be a good professional and there is still a possibility you can get hurt.

The hurt is for everybody, it can happen anytime. When you're in the tube, and you put your hand on the wall and the tunnel throws you, you can tear a ligament. Many others things can happen, so accidents in the sea can happen to anybody. Always surf consciously; you must know what is happening.

What advice do you have for women surfers? *Susana:* Surfing is good for the mind, for the body. It is the best feeling; everybody should try it. Each time you do it, you want more, more. It is a thing you must devote yourself to. It isn't easy; it's difficult. Each day you get a new thing—you are doing a new development.

Tais: You have to go and sacrifice every day: each day there is a novelty, always you are doing a new thing.

The surf action for me, it's a life, peace, ecology, religion—like a thing you have to be.

The surf is all for me. I live on the beach. I have contact with the water, with nature. I am in harmony. I like the calm life and peace, like nature and animals. The surf is life, breath; [it] is all.

Tais: For me, surfing is a vice. But it's a sweet vice.

(Translated from the Portuguese by Cristina Ramos.)

CHAPTER 8

SURFING AND LIBERATION

THE FREEDOM OF NO LIMITS

As youngster, many surfers remember sitting on the beach after a particularly difficult day in the waves. We were cold, chest heaving, the gray of the morning permeating everything. We had days when the ocean was roaring, testing the strength of our arms and our will. Our friends had made it out past the lineup, but after repeated thrashings,

There is treasure in the dragon's cave. But to find it, we must traverse through our limits. Limits are mostly internal barbed wire: our own fears and insecurity getting in the way of our best selves. Limits make us suffer, because it pains us to be fearful and insecure. This is why we strap boards to our ankles and enter into the water—and precisely why you felt so good when you stood up victoriously on that first wave.

> "Letting go gives us freedom, and freedom is the only condition for happiness . . ."—Thich Nhat Hanh

we were too scared and too unsure of ourselves to continue. We could only sit and watch, defeated by our own limits. We knew there would be stories and glances exchanged when our friends returned, but we hated feeling less than, unable, fearful. Why couldn't we make it out?

Facing our fears and insecurities is like walking out of the castle gates to meet the dragon head-on.

As the women in this book have shown us, surfing can be a deep training ground for living beyond our perceived limits and seeing what we're made of. Overcoming limits in water is preparation for overcoming limits on land.

Liane Louie changed careers in mid-life after she realized her surfing dream. Cheryl Larsen began to revise life's possibilities as she returned

to the ocean she both loved and feared. Zeuf let her tears flow into the water as she drew on the power of the sea to overcome breast cancer.

Yet, there are some dark places in the dragon's cave.

Waves can produce great joy, but also great suffering. We hear stories of great ecstasy as well as great pain, even death, when we hear about the power of waves. Then there is the everyday pain or discomfort of getting hit repeatedly by waves, cold shivers down wetsuits, and that acidic feeling you get when you both want and don't want something so badly. This "small suffering" is a metaphor for the big challenges and the "big suffering" in our lives.

To erase limits we go directly to the heart of what frightens us, because through the door of hardship is where our hearts open to joy.

We greet our fear and hardship and just see it as it is. We might say, "Wow, I just got pummeled by that wave." Or, "I'm scared, but I'm still here and I'm still paddling . . ."

As we deal directly with the hardship of being pushed around by Mother Nature—the fear of drowning, or the struggle of being embarrassed about not being good at something—we begin to free ourselves from limitations of fear and insecurity.

With our limits behind us, we move forward and begin to see life as a possibility as opposed to a series of obstacles. As we improve and become freer on waves, we can translate this to the freedom of limitlessness on land. It is so freeing to carve a graceful arc through the heart of a wave, the way that Rell Sunn did, in our hearts. So we keep coming back, despite the fear and hardship, to meet waves and the challenges of our lives head-on.

SURFING: A GIFT TO THE WORLD

One of the greatest maladies of the modern world is feeling scattered from the mentality of multitasking. We miss the joy of a simple meal, the pain of our loved ones, the bliss of a moment—because we are constantly moving to the next worry and the next task. Because we feel scattered, we lose our connection to those around us. We gloss over both our joy and our pain as we try to fill every moment with things to do, things to watch, read, worry about. As a result, we become less effective, less connected, and more anxious. The resultant "noise" in our brains causes great suffering.

Thich Nhat Hanh, a venerated Vietnamese Buddhist, speaks of a solution that is so utterly simple it seems profane.

Be, body and mind, exactly where you are. That is, practice a mindfulness that makes you aware of each moment. Think to yourself, "I am breathing" when you're breathing; "I am anxious" when you're anxious; even, "I am washing the dishes" when you're washing the dishes. To be totally *into* this moment is the goal of mindfulness. Right now is precious and shall never pass this way again.

A wave is a precious moment, amplified: a dynamic natural sculpture that shall never pass this way again. Our interaction with waves—to be fully in the moment, without relationship troubles, bills, or worries—is what frees us. Each moment that we are fully with waves is evidence of our ability to live in the here and now. There *is* nothing else in the universe when you're making that elegant bottom turn.

Here. Now. So simple, but so elusive.

A wave demands your attention. It is very difficult to be somewhere else, in your mind, when there is such a gorgeous creation of nature moving your way. Just being close to waves brings us

closer to being mindful. To surf them is the training ground for mindfulness. The ocean can seem chaotic, like the world we live in. But somehow we're forced to slice through the noise—to paddle around and through the adversities of life and get directly to the joy. This is what we need for liberation.

This is a gift to ourselves. The challenge is, how do you extend the benefits of surfing beyond your time in the water?

Sometimes the bliss of surfing is met with the letdown of being back on land. We walk back to our cars and strap boards to roofs—and slowly the world of car horns, cell phones, and to-do lists creeps back into our consciousness. How long can our ocean high last? This duality is why we sometimes hear of surfers who stray. They become tangled in drugs, unhealthy relationships, and unproductive lives because they cannot integrate the fluidity of ocean life with the rigidity of land life. The wave becomes their drug and the pain of coming down from that high is too much.

If we can be as mindful in our lives as we are when we are catching and riding a wave, we can bring the ocean back with us for the benefit of ourselves and those around us.

If each moment with your partner, your children, or your work were a perfect wave coming your way, would you give the moment only half your attention? Would you stop for a cell phone call just as the wave reached you? To extend the benefits of surfing to our lives is to bring the lesson of mindfulness to the everyday. To focus the way we do when we're stroking into that left-hander is how we make good things happen for us and for those around us. We can take our sea-calmness and come home and sit with our loved ones with full attention. The depth of this kind of listening is both simple and incredibly powerful.

We can take the single-minded focus of riding waves and apply that to our work. This is a focus that goes beyond our distractions and insecurities and revels in the joy of riding.

Focus destroys limits and gets you to what you want.

YOU DESERVE IT

Love yourself enough to surf. And surf often. Love yourself enough to push everything aside as you carve out some time with Mother Ocean. Bring your after-surf glow back home with you and become fluid like water. Your deep attention for yourself and others can be transformational. As we experience success in the water, we build evidence that our success on land is possible. This is how we integrate ourselves.

Some people say surfing is selfish. Yes, surfing is selfish; but we deserve it. If we can use surfing to fulfill our highest potential, then we can also bring the benefits of our mindfulness back to the world.

We give thanks for the gift of surfing.

Aloha.

Boas ondas (Portuguese)—Good waves to you.

ABOUT THE AUTHORS

Mary Osborne

Mary Osborne is the winner of the MTV reality show, *Surf Girls*, and a world-class professional longboarder. She has been featured in *Longboard, Surfing, Surf News, Surfer, Wahine, Surfer's Path,* and *Surfing Girl* magazines, and in many surf films, including *Longboard Magic.* She is the winner of the Action Girl of the Year Award (sponsored by the Action Girl Expo) for 2003.

Kia Afcari

Kia Afcari has been a writer, facilitator, youth-program consultant, columnist, music critic, and photographer. He has surfed for the last twenty years—in places like California, Florida, Hawaii, Brazil, Mexico, and West Africa. He is currently teaching his eight-year-old daughter how to surf and working on his first screenplay.

ABOUT THE
CONTRIBUTORS

Bev Sanders

Bev Sanders has enjoyed over twenty-five years in the action sports industry, beginning as a ski instructor at the age of sixteen. She cofounded Avalanche Snowboards in 1982, and greatly impacted the evolution of the new sport. After devoting herself to the development of women's boarding gear in 1995, *Transworld Magazine* officially recognized Bev's contributions and dedication, honoring her as the Pioneer Woman of Snowboarding. She learned to surf at the age of forty-four, and launched Las Olas Surf Safaris for Women, with the desire to empower women to excel in sports as well as in life.

Elizabeth Pepin

Surf photographer and filmmaker Elizabeth Pepin's images have appeared in numerous museums, galleries, newspapers, and magazines, and in the only book on the history of women's surfing, *Girl in the Curl*. Elizabeth has traveled to Europe, Mexico, and Hawaii to surf and photograph more than four hundred women and girl surfers with both water cameras and from the beach. She has also helped produce more than two dozen programs and has won four Emmy Awards for her television work.

Current projects include surf photographs in *Surf Style*, a surf art book to be published in 2004, coproducing a high-definition documentary on the problems facing California's coast for PBS release, coproducing a half-hour documentary with surfer/filmmaker Sally Lundburg on big wave surfer and scientist Sarah Gerhardt, and writing a San Francisco jazz history/photography book, which will be published by Chronicle Books in 2005.

Liane Louie

Liane Louie is an almost-forty-something novice surfer who has rediscovered herself. She is a former psychologist turned foundation officer for a small foundation in San Francisco. She divides her time between San Francisco and Hawaii. She received her PhD in Clinical Psychology from the Pacific Graduate School of Psychology in Palo Alto, California.

Janine Daley

Janine Daley is a mother, a surfer, and an exercise physiologist. She has an MS in Exercise Physiology, is an ACE (American Council on Exercise) Certified Personal Trainer, a Medical Exercise Specialist, a certified Certified Health Promotion Director (Cooper Institute), and an Advanced Fitness Specialist (Cooper Institute).

APPENDICES

A BRIEF SURFING GLOSSARY

Here are a few of the many terms used by surfers in the United States.

A-FRAME A wave that has a pronounced peak and is breaking both left and right.

BAILING The process of getting off the wave by jumping safely off your board.

BACKSIDE Riding with your back to the face of the wave. For regular-footers, this would be riding a wave that breaks toward the left; for goofy-footers, riding a wave that breaks to the right.

BARREL The hollow portion created by a curling wave (aka, tube, green room, pipe).

BETTY A female surfer, or a beautiful girl.

CLOSEOUT When a wave crashes all at once, not allowing the surfer to ride the face.

CURL The curling lip or top of a wave.

CHOPPY When the ocean surface is bumpy due to the wind.

DING A puncture or abrasion on a surfboard. Surfers hate getting dings.

DROPPING IN The moment that you stand and ride down the face of a wave. Also used thusly, "She totally *dropped in* on me." Meaning that she broke surfing etiquette by riding down the face of a wave that was being ridden by another surfer.

EATING IT Falling off of a wave (aka, wipeout).

FACE The slanted unbroken part of a wave.

FRONTSIDE The opposite of backside, when a surfer is facing the face of the wave. Riding toward the left for a goofy-footer or riding toward the right for a regular-footer.

GLASSY When the ocean surface is smooth due to a lack of wind (aka, clean)

GOOFY-FOOTER Someone who naturally prefers riding a surfboard with her left foot toward the back of the board.

HANG TEN A longboarding trick where the surfer walks all the way to the nose of the board and places all ten toes over the edge (cheater-five is the same thing, except with only five toes over the edge).

IMPACT ZONE The area in the surf where the waves curl and break. If you paddle out far enough, you can make it past the impact zone.

KICKOUT The graceful way of getting off a wave by turning your board abruptly off the top of the wave.

KOOK A derogatory term for a novice or wannabe surfer.

LINEUP The area of the break where surfers line up to catch waves.

MAKING IT When you are able to outrun the whitewater by surfing ahead of it.

MUSHY When the waves are spilling over and have little steepness.

OFF THE LIP A shortboarding trick where the surfer goes to the top of the wave and makes a quick, sharp turn.

PEAK The highest point of a wave.

PEARLING When the nose of your board goes underwater when you're trying to catch a wave (an embarrassing situation for every surfer).

POP-UP The process of moving from a lying-down position to standing on the board in one graceful motion.

REGULAR-FOOTER Someone who naturally prefers riding a surfboard with her right foot toward the back of the board.

SHOULDER The unbroken area just beside the broken part of a wave.

SOUP The frothy area in front of a broken wave.

STOKE The feeling of happiness you get from surfing (i.e., "I was so stoked!").

STRINGER The wooden strip that runs down the center of a surfboard.

WOMEN-FOCUSED SURF SCHOOLS

How to find a great surf school

By Claude Silver, girlsAdventureOUT

In 2002, JudeAnn Smith and I founded girlsAdventureOUT. We started as a company that offered surfing clinics exclusively to women. We've learned that women-focused surf schools tend to offer a fun and supportive way to learn how to surf. Over the course of our first year in business, we had a number of inquiries to broaden our reach to men, children, and educational institutions. In April of 2003, we announced the expansion of our surfing camps and clinics to men, kids, educational institutions, and corporations. In the past two and a half years, we have taught approximately a thousand people from all over the world to surf! We strive to create an empowering, nurturing, and safe atmosphere for all of our students.

Ratio of students to teachers:
We believe that the best ratio is 3:1 (students to teacher). The maximum should be 4:1. This allows for a lot of one-on-one coaching, as well as the camaraderie of a small group.

Experience of teachers:
Find out what the experience is of the teachers who will be your instructors. Are the instructors simply surfers, or are they actually teachers who get inspired by empowering others to learn how to surf? Many people can surf—but it is a special person who can teach, coach, cheerlead, *and* surf.

Demographics of students:
What is the typical age of the students? Will you be learning with kids, adults, or just women? Go with what feels most comfortable for you.

Gear:
What is included in your school? Will everyone have his or her own board to use? How about a wetsuit and booties (if needed)?

Curriculum:
What will you be learning? You want to learn more than just proper positioning and how to stand. Ask questions! How about safety and surfing etiquette? You want to learn about wave structure and breaks, timing and balance on the board, how to choose the best waves for you, etc.

Insurance:
Ask if the school is insured. Liability insurance is expensive for schools to purchase, but so necessary. Make sure you ask all the potential schools you check out if they have their own liability insurance for surfing.

Women's surf schools

Note: *New surf schools are opening all the time. This list was compiled in the fall of 2004.*

Big Island Girl Surf
Makahiki Adventures
PO Box 10452
Hilo, HI 96721 USA
(808) 326–0269
www.bigislandgirlsurf.com

Danger Woman
Surf City Surfing Lessons
PO Box 3013
Huntington Beach, CA 92605 USA
(714) 898–2088
www.dangerwoman.com

EasyDrop Surf Camp Itacaré
Rua João Coutinho, 140
Centro Itacaré
Bahia, Brazil
45.530-000 (*zip code*)
(55) 73 251 3065
www.easydrop.com

Florida Surf Lessons
(various locations in Florida)
(561) 625–5375
www.floridasurflessons.com

girlsAdventureOUT
1750 Francisco Blvd., Suite 5
Pacifica, CA 94044 USA
(650) 557–0641
www.girlsadventureout.com

HB Wahine
301 Main St., Suite 102
Huntington Beach, CA 92648 USA
(714) 969–9399
www.hbwahine.com

Kelea Surf Spa
(spas in Hawaii & Costa Rica)
PO Box 974
San Clemente, CA 92674 USA
(949) 492–SAND
www.keleasurfspa.com

Las Olas Surf Safaris for Women
(Mexico)
991 Tyler St. #101
Benicia, CA 94510 USA
(707) 746–6435
www.surflasolas.com

Maui Surfer Girls
& SwellWoman
PO Box 1158
Puunene, HI 96784 USA
(866) MSG–2002, (808) 579–8211
www.mauisurfergirls.com
www.swellwoman.com

SurfHER (Linda Benson)
PO Box 235336
Encinitas, CA 92023 USA
(760) 749–5997
www.surfher.net

Surf Honeys
Inniscrone, Ireland
353 (87) 8399528
353 (86) 8376270
www.surfhoneys.com

Surf Sisters
Natural Art Showroom
2370 S. Atlantic Ave.
Cocoa Beach, FL 32931 USA
(321) 783–0764
nashop@earthlink.net

Surf Sister Surf School
Box 6
Tofino, BC Canada V0R 2Z0
(877) 724–7873
www.surfsister.com

Wahine Adventures
(adventures in Mexico, Costa Rica, and
Washington State)
www.wahinesurf.com

WB Surf Camp
530 Causeway Drive
Suite B-1
Wrightsville Beach, NC 28480 USA
1–866–361–GIRL
www.wbsurfcamp.com

Yesco Girls Surf School
(Japan)
www.surfmedia-tk.co.jp/yesco_club.html

*Note: The above listings are for informational
purposes only. They do not represent an
endorsement of the above surf schools.*

OTHER RESOURCES FOR WOMEN SURFERS

Organizations

Boarding for Breast Cancer
6230 Wilshire Blvd. #179
Los Angeles, CA 90048 USA
(323) 571–2197
www.b4bc.org

LA Surf Bus (Surf Academy)
811 N. Catalina Ave., Suite 2316
Redondo Beach, CA 90277 USA
(877) 599–SURF (7873)
www.surfacademy.org/surfbus/

League of Women Surfers
Mary Setterholm
Surf Academy
811 N. Catalina Ave., Suite 2316
Redondo Beach, CA 90277 USA
(310) 372–2790
www.womensurfers.org

The Surfrider Foundation
P.O. Box 6010
San Clemente, CA 92674-6010 USA
(800) 743–SURF
www.surfrider.org

Ride A Wave
PO Box 7606
Santa Cruz, CA 95061 USA
(831) 239–3672
www.rideawave.org

Sisters of the Sea
Jacksonville, FL USA
www.sistersofthesea.org

Surf Aid International
555 Second St., #5
Encinitas, CA 92024 USA
(760) 753–1103
www.surfaidinternational.org

Surfers Medical Association
PO Box 1210
Aptos, CA 95001 USA
Smacentral@aol.com
www.damoon.net/sma/index

Source books

Barks, Coleman and Michael Green. *The Illuminated Rumi.* Broadway Books, 1997.

Gabbard, Andrea. *Girl in the Curl: A Century of Women's Surfing.* Seal Press, 2000.

Goldberg, Natalie. *Writing Down the Bones: Freeing the Writer Within.* Shambhala Publications, 1986.

Gorman, Jack M., ed. *Fear and Anxiety: The Benefits of Translational Research.* American Psychiatric Association, 2004.

Jackins, Harvey. *The Human Side of Human Beings: The Theory of Re-Evaluation Counseling.* Rational Island Publishers, 1994.

Nhat Hanh, Thich. *The Heart of the Buddha's Teaching.* Broadway Books, 1999.

Perry, Bruce. *Memories of Fear: How the Brain Stores and Retrieves Physiologic States, Feelings, Behaviors and Thoughts from Traumatic Events.* (Academy version from *Splintered Reflections: Images of the Body in Trauma,* Edited by J. Goodwin and R. Attias. New York, NY: Basic Books, 1999.

Warren, Lee E. *The Negative Effect of Fear on the Mind, Part I.* Plim Report, Vol. 12 (3), 2003.

Yao, Moses. *Togodoo: A Pathwalk with the African Thirteen Moon Cycles.* Morningstar Communications, 1994.

Magazines

Fluir Girls
(Brazil)
www2.uol.com.br/fluir/fluir_girls/index

Pacific Longboarder
(Australia)
(07) 5448 1354
www.pacificlongboarder.com

Surf Life for Women
3052 N. Main Street
Morro Bay, CA 93442 USA
(805) 772–6896
www.surflifeforwomen.com

SG Magazine
950 Calle Amanecer, Suite C
San Clemente, CA 92673 USA
www.sgmag.com

SurfGirl Magazine (Carve)
(United Kingdom)
carve@orcasurf.co.uk
www.orcasurf.co.uk/data/
  carve/carve_gsurfing/girlsurfing

The Surfers Journal
PO Box 4006
San Clemente, CA 92674 USA
(949) 361–0331
www.surfersjournal.com

Waves Surfgirl
PO Box 1014, Haymarket NSW 1240
Australia
(02) 9581 9400

Water

(USA)

(800) 849–8754

gina@waterzine.com

www.waterzine.com

Women-focused surf shops

Aquahine Surf Shop

3689 Mission Blvd

San Diego, CA 92109 USA

(858) 488–8181

info@aquahine.com

www.aquahine.com

The Girl Next Door Surf Shop

1020 Anastasia Blvd.

St. Augustine, FL 32084 USA

(904) 461–1441

www.surf-station.com/gnd

Paradise Surf Shop

3961 Portola Drive

Santa Cruz, CA 95062 USA

(831) 462–3880

www.paradisesurf.com

Surfmom

www.surfmom.com

Salty Sister Surf Shop

2796 Carlsbad Blvd.

Carlsbad, CA 92008 USA

(760) 434–1122

Rocker Board Shop

12204 Venice Boulevard

Mar Vista, CA 90066 USA

(310) 397–8300

www.rockerboardshop.com

Surfing art and culture

Beach Party Paintings—Surf art by Shannon Wing

Blue Crush—The original women's surf film by Bill Ballard

Blue Crush—Hollywood movie release by Universal Studios

Heart—Women's surf film with Kassia Meador, Prue Jeffries, and Sophia Mulanavich

Heart of the Sea—Documentary on the life of surfing legend Rell Sunn

Martha Jenkins Surf Gallery—Photos of top female surfers

JoyfulArt.net—Surf illustrations and ocean murals by Teresa Gemora

Poetic Silence—A women's 16mm surf film by Bill Ballard

Roxy Learn to Surf, Now—Surfing DVD presented by Roxy

Surfer's Journal *Biographies: Greats of Women's Surfing*—Female surf legends on DVD

http://www.shannonsurf.com/—Surf art by
Shannon McIntyre
7 Girls—DVD starring Megan Abubo, Rochelle
Ballard, Keala Kennelly, Layne Beachley
Listings courtesy of www.boardfolio.com

Surf-industry manufacturers

Mary Osborne's Sponsors:

Mary's Sponsors

BettyBelts

www.bettybelts.com

Etnies

www.etniesgirl.com

Freestyle Watches

www.freestyleusa.com

JamCore Training

www.jamcoretraining.com

MKA Capital Group INC

http://www.mkacap.com/

Robert August Surfboards

www.robertaugust.com

Sexwax

www.sexwax.com

Surf One Girl

http://surf-one-girl.com/

Other manufacturers

Leila Lei—Jewelry

Aaron Chang—Clothing

American Wave—Wetuits to fit your body,
budget, and lifestyle

BettyBelts—Hand-sewn shell belts, made of all
natural materials

Billabong—Clothing

Blink—Clothing

Body Code—Clothing

Body Glove—Wetsuits, clothing

Bungalow Beach Designs—Surf and beach home
decor, bedding, accessories

Chicks Who Rip—Clothing

Chicky Bumps—Surf wax

Cover Style—Swimwear

Dawls—Clothing

DC Shoes—Footwear

Déesse—Clothing

Dickies—Clothing

Disciple Clothing—Clothing for girls

Divine Eyewear—Eyewear

Dreamwave—Surf bedding and blankets in
Hawaiian print styles

Finch Swimwear—Clothing

Flojos—Footwear

Fox Racing—Clothing

Free Style—Watches

Gallaz—Shoes

GlassyGreen—Rash guards and waterwear

Gravis Footwear—Footwear

Headhunter—Sunscreen products

Hele—Surf-inspired Tahitian black pearl
necklaces

Hobie—Clothing, eyewear

HotGirls—Clothing

Hula Angel—Clothing

Indo Board—Balance trainer

Lucy Love—Clothing

Maui Style—Clothing for *na wahine*

Miken—Clothing

Nice Footwear—Footwear

Nikita—Clothing

O'Neill—Clothing, wetsuits

OP—Clothing

Point Conception—Clothing

Reef—Footwear

Ride Naked SurfStyles—Free expressions for women and kids

Rip Curl—Clothing, wetsuits

Roxy—Clothing

Robert August Surfboards—surfboards

Rusty—Clothing, surfboards

Saltrock Surfwear—Clothing and wetsuits for women

Sea Angel—Clothing

Shannon Surf—Surfboards by Shannon McIntyre

SueNami Surf Co.—Clothing

Surf Angel—Clothing

Surf Chick—Clothing

Surf Mom—Surf products for the whole family

Surfer Chicks—Hawaiian accessories, jewelry

Trixie Surfboards—Surfboards exclusively for women and girls, clothing

Tropical Winds—Beach blankets

Uhula.com—Bedding for beachgoers

Velvet Eyewear—Eyewear

Volcom—Clothing

Von Zipper—Eyewear

Wahine Wax—Surfboard wax

Xpression Wetsuits—Wetsuits for junior girls

Listings courtesy of www.boardfolio.com

INDEX